Cruising by Mailboat

History, Culture and Adventure in the Bahama Islands

By Captain Fred Braman, USN(ret)

*With Photographs by Dave Blake
and Paintings by Randy Curry*

Travel Adventures
Sketches of Bahamian History and Culture
How to Travel Instructions
Travel and Schedule Information
Over 150 Color Photographs

"Travel throughout The Bahamas in a new and interesting way. Learn about this wonderful country, visit the little places and meet the real Bahamians."

1

Cover Photographs by Dave Blake Photography.

Front Cover: MailBoat *Fiesta Mail* while docked at Potters Cay, Nassau, and taken from a bridge connecting Nassau and Paradise Island. Permission to use the photo was granted by the ship's owner, Captain Elvin Taylor.

Back Cover: A modern *MailBoat,* designed and built for the mailboat trade, is pictured while being loaded at Potters Cay with Mega-Resorts on nearby Paradise Island as a backdrop.

ISBN: 978-0-578-71114-0

Library of Congress Control Number: 2020925882

Published by DiggyPod in the USA

Acknowledgements

First and Foremost Louise: My wife of over a half century who still lets me go off on these strange adventures, though she'd prefer that I play more golf!

The Kruse Family: Daughter Monica, Son-in-Law Matt, Grandson Grant and Granddaughter Madchen, who put up with Grandpa's stories and offered a comment or two plus technical help and advice.

Arlene Wiltse: the best Sister-in-Law ever who knows nothing of this, but, is a great proofreader!

My MailBoat Companions: Dave Blake, Phil Lugger, Jim Zoller, Mike Schmidt, Jack Hundertmark, Don McAvoy, Perry McDonald and Olga Copson who experienced these adventures with me and made them come to life.

Steve Morrell, Editor of Southwinds Magazine: Steve has been supportive of my writing and has taught me a lot, for which I am grateful. He published much of the material in this book as magazine articles.

Volunteer Editors Perry McDonald and **Doc Savage:** old friends and always my first readers.

Kendra Whylly: Administrative Assistant of the Dean Shipping Company of Nassau, who was my go-to person for questions.

Many Many Bahamians met along the way who made all this special.

"The beauty of these Islands surpasses that of any others."

Christopher Columbus, 1492

Major Contributors

When I started this project, I was no stranger to The Bahamas. To supplement my over thirty years of personal experience, I read a lot of books, studied scientific articles, subscribed to Bahamian publications, and searched on-line sites for more information. I was also fortunate and privileged to meet professionals who knew the islands well, loved them as I did, and wrote about their history and of mailboats. In addition, I rode a lot of mailboats myself with friends. My intent is to inform future adventurers about a really fun and interesting way to visit a great country and how to do it. The majority of this book are renditions of personal experiences, for which the only references are my personal notes. My book is a "popular" rather than "scholarly" work. I did not search museum archives, wade through library stacks of historical files, nor do the hard work of original research. Portions of the book that describe the history of the country and of mailboats depend on the efforts of a few real professionals who did all that very hard, scholarly work. They have been incredibly sharing of their work and encouraging of mine. Additionally, the illustrations of mailboats, past and present, make the book come to life. Historical boat images are captured by a talented artist and modern boat images and the travel adventures themselves by a talented photographer. Here also, I am indebted to the work of others. There are many who contributed to my background and general knowledge and are cited in the bibliography. However, there are four professionals who contributed to this book in extraordinary ways, giving of their work, talent, advice and support, just by being asked. There would be no book without them. Here is a little about them, their work and their contributions.

Eric Wiberg: *Author's note: Due to their importance, all historians of the Bahamas discuss mailboats, and I have learned from many. Eric Wiberg has been instrumental in my mailboat education and most of my writing about them has his thumbprint. Additionally, he has been extremely supportive of my work. As a true maritime historian and author, he has to his credit many volumes about maritime history, mailboats included. He is without question the foremost authority on Bahamian mailboats. His expansive works can be found at Amazon. See also www.ericwiberg.com.*

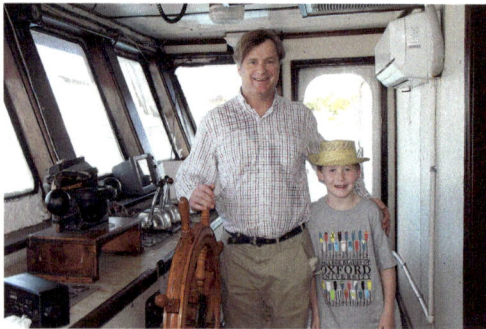

Eric and son, Felix Perkin Dunmore Wiberg, a youthful mailboat veteran by 12!

Eric Wiberg was raised in Cable Beach, Nassau. An experienced mariner with 75,000 miles under his nautical belt, Eric has operated boats from yachts to tankers across oceans and has four round-the-world voyages to his credit, visiting over 70 countries on six continents in the process. He was licensed as a captain (1995), and in maritime law (2005) and has earned a masters degree in marine affairs. He worked afloat for a salvage firm in Freeport and spent five years marketing tugboats from Manhattan and four years in maritime media. Eric has studied at six universities in three countries, including Oxford, New York, and Lisbon. He is the author of over a dozen books of nautical non-fiction, six focused on the Bahamas. His research has helped locate the remains of US,

Norwegian, German and Italian WW II servicemen, leading to posthumous military awards. He has published over 3 million words and appeared in four documentaries and TV programs. His writing has been translated into Spanish, Norwegian, Danish, and Portuguese, and his research is held in archives in the US, Bermuda, Bahamas, Cuba, and Uruguay. Since the early 1980s, he has voyaged or flown to all but two of the major Bahamian islands and has a special affinity for Northern Eleuthera and Southern Abaco. Son Felix's middle name is Dunmore, for the town on Harbour Island. A citizen of the United States and the European Union, Eric is based in Boston.

Steve Dodge: *Author's note: As a lifelong sailor, I've long been acquainted with the work of Steve Dodge. Among sailors, he is best known as the author of "The Cruising Guide to Abaco, Bahamas," a work I have known well in my thirty years of Abaco sailing. Though I have long been guided through Bahamian waters by Steve, it was another of his works, "Abaco, The History of an Out Island and its Cays," that helped spur my interest in both mailboats and Bahamas history in general. His work is well represented in this book. Author and publisher of many publications about the Bahamas, his work can be viewed at www.wspress.com.*

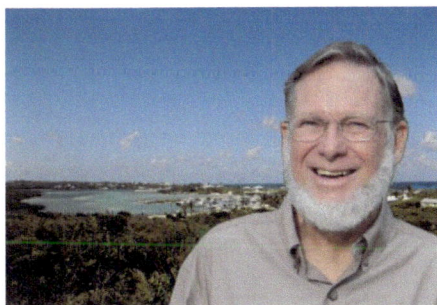

Steve and his White Sound home in the background

Steve Dodge is Professor of History Emeritus at Millikin University, Decatur, Illinois. He earned a Ph.D. from the University of Minnesota in Latin American History and did his early research and writing on Venezuela. Steve is a sailor and first visited Abaco in 1973. He soon became interested in the history of the area. During the late 1970s he began research for a history of Abaco and also built a summer residence at White Sound three miles south of Hope Town on Elbow Cay. *The History of an Out Island and its Cays* was first published in 1983; second and third editions were published in 1995 and 2005 (the third edition is still in print). He has also written (with Vernon Malone) *A Guide and History of Hope Town* and served as editorial advisor for *The Bahamas Index and Yearbook,* which was published annually from 1986 to 2002. In 1989 he published the first edition of *The Cruising Guide to Abaco, Bahamas*, an annually updated guide now in its 31st year. He owns a couple of outboard boats used for hydrographic research for the cruising guide, but lost his venerable 1970 Morgan 28 sailboat in Hurricane Dorian. He divides his time between White Sound and New Smyrna Beach, Florida.

Dave Blake: *Author's note: Dave, a great friend since we were both eighteen year old college freshmen, has been riding mailboats as long as I have. How wonderful it is to have an old friend who will do these trips with me and is also a talented photographer able to capture all of it. Dave (aka, Kink) takes photographs of things nobody else will think of taking. Readers will agree that his photographs bring this book to life. He has a lot more to share with his art. Check out his site below.*

Dave Blake, a mid-westerner by both birth and upbringing, heeded the often cited relocation cry, "go Southwest young man, go Southwest," or something like that! He and wife Carmen relocated to the sunny Southwest and since 1981 have called Scottsdale, Arizona home. After a successful career in the Aerospace Industry, Dave retired in 2005 to live the good life. Dave had a history of loving photography and took it up in earnest following retirement. When he's not taking time out to ride Bahamian mailboats, Dave and Carmen can often be found on long automobile road trips, photographing "Americana," as he finds it "through his lens." Their frequent road trips have covered both the nation's heartland as well as North

Dave and his camera

America's extremities including the Alaskan Highway and the Canadian Northeast Maritime provinces. If there is a favorite trip, Route 66 may well be it with relics from past generations. Roadside oddities (world's largest ball of string, Muffler Men), and historical locations are among his favorite subjects. Dave and Carmen are also Blues music fans and Dave has artist album covers to his credit. He also photographs medical missions to Central and South America, to which he and his retired nurse wife are frequent volunteers. Dave views the world as his canvas and really enjoys capturing the unusual. He uses Canon cameras and lenses. View some of his work in this book and more at http://www.pbasc.com/twolanetommy/.

Randy Curry: *Author's note: Randy is a multi-talented artist who can create just about any type of art. Historic mailboats can't be photographed, but old, grainy, black and white photos are available to paint. Randy has brought them back to life in colorful renditions of yesteryear. As you will read, he has a good pedigree for painting mailboats. His family and friends have been*

9

associated with them for decades.

Randy with samples of his art. His paintings of historic Mailboats are in Chapter 3.

Randy Curry of Green Turtle Cay, Abaco, Bahamas has been a self-employed artist for almost 40 years. He sold his first acrylic painting at the age of 13 to a visitor from Germany. This encouraged him to continue painting and he soon graduated to oils. Expanding his art over the years, Randy is now a painter, wood carver, sign artist, graphic designer, photographer and videographer. Growing up in the Abaco Islands, there was no shortage of beautiful scenery to paint. Over the past four decades, he has sold hundreds of paintings and wood carvings to visitors from all over the world. Randy is probably best known for his solid mahogany, relief carvings, a unique combination of a hand carving and hand painting. Always growing artistically, Randy's newest works combine digital painting with traditional painting done by hand. He offers Giclée prints that are hand embellished for texture and depth with traditional oil paints and brushes, and finally protected with multiple clear UV coatings for a fade-proof result. Randy produces a wide range of quality art. If you have a project, he can probably do it. Contact Randy and see his art at: www.yessy.com/randycurry.

Forward

A lifelong sailor tried a different way to cruise the Bahamas - Mail Boats! Spared from the navigation duties and weather planning required of cruising sailors, mailboats brought their own set of travel challenges. It all turned into a grand adventure for this sailor and old friends, septuagenarians all! I've had this idea for some time. I first noticed mailboats while sailing along the Bahamian out-islands during a long trip. No matter how small the island, it seemed that the mailboat would come in while I was there. Here is how I described it in my 2013 book, *Too Old Not to Go* about my voyage.

"After a great week, my stay at Great Harbour Cay in the Berry Islands was over. I made one more trip to my favorite beach, turned in the dilapidated pink jeep I had rented, and topped Rhombus off with water, fuel, and some needed supplies. Luckily, the Bahamas mailboat had docked in the town the previous day and the stores were full of supplies. Mailboats are the link to the larger world for the small, outer islands and they carry everything - milk, beer, groceries, lumber, crates of chickens, pallets of canned goods, goats, passengers, and even mail. A cruise by mailboat is now on my list of fun things to try; flexible schedule required!"

The Mailboat idea lay dormant for five years before finally emerging for real consideration. I knew basically how the system worked, but needed a lot more information to actually make a plan. I also needed "cruising companions." Mailboats begin their journey at Potters Cay, a small shipping point between Nassau and Paradise Island. Mailboats cover the entire Bahamas chain, visiting one or two islands before returning to Nassau and repeating the schedule the next week. Today, around twenty moderately sized mailboats depart from Potters Cay, and make weekly out-island trips to over 50 destinations. There are several larger boats that have more frequent schedules, but fewer destinations, and ferries with daily departures and returns to the most demanded localities. All the boats carry people, cargo, and mail. You can go anywhere in The Bahamas by boat!

Captain Gurth Dean docks at Great Harbour Cay, Berry Islands, Bahamas, during a 2012 sailing trip. I watched people as well as cargo get off. I watched people get off the same boat in the same spot in 2018. In 2020, I got off!!

Having acquired a little more information about cruising possibilities, my attention turned to "cruising companions." Who do I know that has the time and is actually "crazy enough to do this with me?" I phrased my request just that way to two old college friends who immediately came back with, "I'm in!!!" A few weeks later, Dave Blake arrived from Arizona and Phil Lugger arrived from Michigan, and we all met in Nassau to begin our adventure. A short time later, we did it again, this time with more participants. I think you'll find it all different, interesting, and fun. In the coming pages, I'll describe mailboats, mailboat travel, a little about the archipelago's formation, Bahamian history and culture, discuss a few historical mailboats, and introduce one iconic mailboat family. Since MailBoat travel is an adventure into the real Bahamas among real Bahamians, included are a few *"Bahamian Interludes,"* short stories of Bahamian history and culture, as we encounter them during our travels.

My goals for readers are simple: learn something about The Bahamas and mailboats, enjoy and partake in our adventures, and maybe go yourself! Now I'll tell you all about it!

Table of Contents

Bahamian Interludes

Stories of History, Geology and Culture

Chapter 1: The Bahama Islands
Geology of the Archipelago

The beauty of the Bahama Islands from space is striking! Up close and personal it's even better. For me, two thousand and twenty marked over thirty years of travel to The Bahamas. Most of my visits have been in my own cruising sailboats, *Monilou* and *Rhombus*, but also by cruise ship, an occasional airplane, and now, by MailBoat! I've lost track of the number of my visits. I've learned to love the country and its people as a second home and have developed over time a deep respect and great awe for the country's extraordinary geography. The 700 islands and over 2000 rocks and cays are sprinkled over 100,000 square miles of ocean. They look like a series of unimposing, low-slung islands from a distance. Close up, especially when you are trying to sail among them, you appreciate the islands' craggy shorelines and gentle beaches, gigantic rocks that jut from otherwise broad open bays, underwater coral traps for the unwary mariner, vast luminous aquamarine sandy banks, deep-blue underwater cliffs, and in-shore blue holes where you can step off a sandy beach into seven hundred feet of water. This NASA photograph from space illustrates the extraordinary geography of this spectacular archipelago. The color contrasts, indicating vastly different depths, are striking and raise difficult questions regarding the islands' formation.

How did the Bahama Islands come to be?

A Geological History (Sort of!):

The Bahamas seem an aberration against nature. In the otherwise deep, deep ocean blue, why suddenly

are there these islands and the grand shallow banks
that accompany them? There is no underwater volcano
with a moving plate in the Earth's crust passing
overhead, such as what created the Hawaiian Islands.
Why then the Bahamas? I've read several accounts of
the Bahama's formation. I'm no geologist, but I'm not
sure that I believe everything I read. Then again, I'm no

geologist. The islands' formation continues to be studied. To this writer, the certainty on the veracity scale of the various Bahamas creation theories lies somewhere south of "Global warming!"

The islands and cays (pronounced "key," derived from ka or ke of the Taino language meaning small islands), are generally long and narrow and oriented Northwest to Southeast along the eastern edges of the Little and Great Bahama Banks. The main exception is Andros, the largest island, located along the very deep and geologically strange "Tongue of the Ocean." The generally accepted theory of formation (super concise version) goes something like this: The break-up of the supercontinent Pangea (Greek for "all Earth"), tectonic plate movement, subduction zones, organic material compacted into limestone rock, sand producing erosion of coral and shells, and even recently theorized Saharan dust (really!), all conspired to form the Bahama Islands. One account from a scientifically reputable source describes the Bahama's formation as part of the Pangea break-up, where pieces of the world as we know it moved to their current locations, propelled along by convection currents in the mantle (molten rock just below the Earth's crust). Another source contends that subsurface rocks were originally part of Africa and rotated into their current place by a means yet to be discovered. Another popular view among geologists states that the Bahamas were never part of Pangea and were formed after the supercontinent drifted apart. The familiar "jigsaw puzzle" fit of the Americas with Africa and Europe, does not work if the Little and Great Bahama Banks are included. Geologists consider shallows much deeper than the Banks to be "land." Today the dry islands are a negligible land mass, but they occupy a large plateau of submarine mountains. While at today's sea level, the Bahama Banks (from Baja

Mar "Shallow Sea") are only forty feet and less below the water's surface, the mountains themselves are up to 14,000 feet above the surrounding ocean floor. For comparison, Mount Washington, the highest point on the Atlantic Seaboard is 6,200 feet above sea level. A fairly recently proffered theory contends that huge boulders, found on top of terrain hundreds of thousands of years younger, were swept from the ocean floor and deposited where they are now located by a sort of primordial surf. This surf was a hundred feet high and travelled at over sixty miles per hour!

So, if not an original part of Pangea, then how did the Bahama Islands develop? Though still debated, most geologists believe that the initial formation, called basement rocks, resulted from the subduction (one of the Earth's plates pulled under another), or in the Bahama's case, the collision of the North American plate with the Caribbean plate. There is general agreement that since the initial "basement" was formed, sedimentary deposits have continued to add to the Bahamian Archipelago, even as the dense "basement" continues to sink. Organic material compacted into limestone added about an inch every thousand years, or about 12,000 feet over the past 140 million years. That's close to depths recorded on today's nautical charts in the deep areas off the Bahama Banks. All this takes lots of time. In human terms, Steve Dodge points out that less than one-half inch has been added since the time of Columbus' voyage. Recent studies indicate that the Bahama formation may have been accelerated by iron rich Saharan dust blown across the Atlantic, which acted as a "fertilizer" for calcium carbonate precipitation. Calcium carbonate is a major component of limestone. As is typical with coral formations, the islands formed on the windward or Atlantic Ocean side of the Banks. This has resulted in dramatic, rocky cliffs

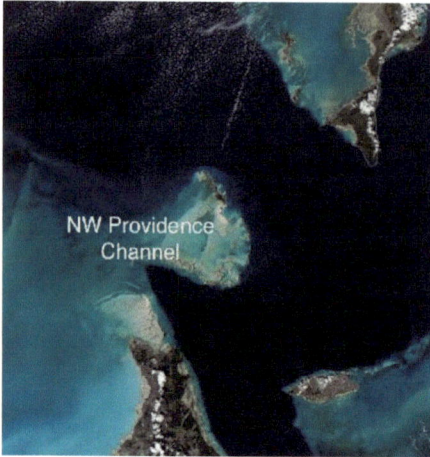

on eastern shores and gentle beaches, shallows, and mangroves in the west. The island landscapes visible today were shaped by the accumulation of carbonate sediments and erosion caused by wind and sea water.

So, why am I a little skeptical of all this?

The NW Providence Channel Passage (the pointed end at the deep blue "V") is one of the places in the Bahamas where sailing off an underwater cliff is vividly illustrated. During a recent voyage in my sloop *Rhombus*, eighteen foot depths near the lone tower marking the pass became 466 feet (the last depth my depth sounder could capably read) in three boat lengths! The real depth according to navigational charts is about 5000 feet and it descends sharply from there. This shallow to suddenly very deep transition happens throughout the Bahamas. How can sediments pile up so steeply and skip adjacent deep-water gaps? Then again, I'm no geologist!

The Bahamas Today:

Regardless of how they were formed, the end result is a country of hundreds of islands that occupies thousands of square miles of ocean. In the 1950s, the United States spent a pile of money connecting forty-eight contiguous states that were already connected by a highway system. There is no question that the improved connectivity of the Interstate Highway System has been a major contributor to the US economy ever since. Economic imperatives drove that huge US national investment, and the improved quality of life for generations of residents is incalculable. But, to achieve the same goals, how do you connect the inhabited Bahamian Islands distributed over 100,000 square miles of ocean? Lots of bridges? I don't think so. Mailboats!

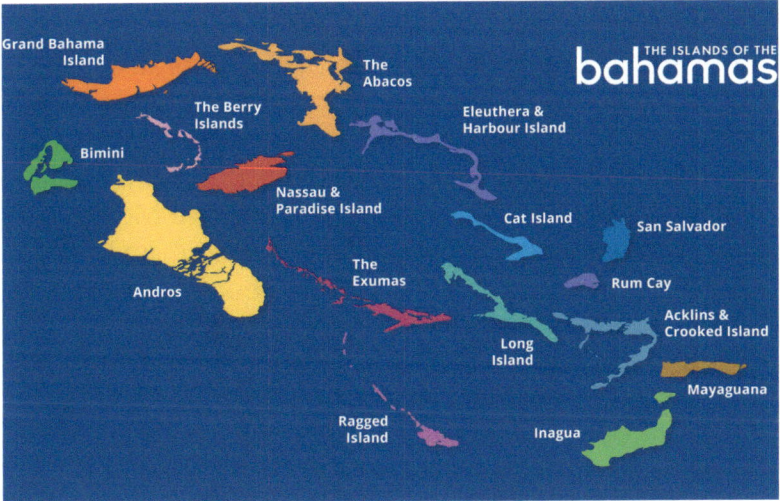

The Islands of The Bahamas cover a big piece of the Atlantic Ocean.

Chapter 2: Why Mailboats?
A Little History

History, geography and eventually the need to improve commerce influenced the coming of mailboats. It didn't happen quickly.

Brief Bahamian History (Very Brief!):

Like all of the New World, settlement of the Caribbean is a fairly recent event. The celebrated Asia-America migration eventually reached Central America and the nearby Islands of the Greater Antilles followed later. The initial "Antillean" settlers of Cuba, Jamaica, Hispaniola and Puerto Rico had a distinctive Mongolian look. The Bahamas was not a "hot property" for settlement, even among indigenous peoples. Eventually, Arawaks from South America, later called Taino, absorbed the Antilleans and wandered north, first to the Caicos Islands and then with forays into the Southern Bahamas. While a few folks popped into the Bahama Islands over the millennia, about 500 A.D. the Lucayans (from Lukku-Cairi, meaning island people) arrived from other Caribbean islands, becoming the Bahamas first substantial human population. Gentile and industrious people with a distinctly oriental appearance, the Lucayans built utopia-like communities throughout the Bahama Archipelago. They stayed for about a thousand years, until the arrival of the Spaniards. Soon after, the native population either died of European diseases, or were carted off to other locales as slaves. Ponce de Leon, in his celebrated tour through Bahama and Florida in 1513, found only one remaining native Lucayan. In a brief moment in time the Lucayans were erased from this Earth, and unfortunately have left few meaningful reminders of their tenure. The islands were empty of human population for the next 135 years and modern Bahamians have no cultural or physical connection to these early residents.

By the mid-1600s the English started to look to the Bahama Islands for settlement. The same religious freedom pressures that sent the Pilgrims to Virginia resulted in new settlements in the Bahamas. The first of the new settlers immigrated to the island they named Eleuthera, Greek for freedom. Settlements on New Providence Island quickly followed and Nassau soon became the center of the English Bahamas. The islands' population grew slowly until the American Revolution, after which "Loyalist," English populations of the former colonies, sought new homes in the Bahamas, Jamaica, Nova Scotia, or England. The Loyalists who re-settled in the Bahamas gave the country's population a boost. They brought their culture with them, which is clearly evident today. Nassau still dominates in terms of

Dave Blake Photography

New Plymouth on Green Turtle Cay looks like a New England fishing village reflecting its "Loyalist" settlers.

population. Freeport and nearby West End on Grand Bahama Island have grown as population centers, taking advantage of their close proximity to the United States for both trade and tourism. Cooperstown and Marsh Harbour on Great Abaco Island are smaller population centers, but these five locations have eighty percent of today's population. Bahamians, however, are spread out. Less than forty of the 700 islands and cays in the archipelago are populated and nearly twenty percent of the population is distributed across the Bahamian map; less than 400 residents in Grand Cay in the far Northwest corner of the country, around a 100 residents in Rum Cay in the center, and about 70 residents in the Ragged Islands in the far south. There are a lot of little "bergs" in the Bahamas!

Throughout its history, The Bahamas has had close ties to the somewhat nefarious, but traditional Bahamian economic activities of pirating, wrecking (the salvage of ships wrecked on nearby reefs), blockade running of Confederate ports during the US Civil War, and bootlegging during US Prohibition. The islands were well situated for all of these activities. Pirates who knew the waters and the area's many navigational hazards found safe haven and at one time were the majority of the population. Steve Dodge suggests in his *Abaco, The History of an Out Island and its Cays,* that "there remain a few drops of pirate blood in all Bahamians."

Wrecking was also a prominent occupation for about two hundred years. Southbound sailing cargo ships from US ports traveled east of Bahama to escape the northerly flow of the Gulf Stream, often finding themselves "wrecked" on barrier reefs lining the fringes of the archipelago. Wrecked ships became subject to local rescue at the price of their cargo. During the era before lighthouses, almost every able bodied Bahamian man was engaged in wrecking. Pirates were eventually run off, lighthouses were built that ruined wrecking as an occupation, and new opportunities during the US Civil War and Prohibition, came and went. As the country grew and the population increased over a wider geographic area, the need to transition to normal economic activity became apparent.

For everyday living, not much was grown or made in the islands. Bahamians who had something to sell, such as a cargo of fish or spiny lobster, or needed manufactured goods themselves to live, had to get them to or from Nassau. As early as 1804, the Bahamas had established some semblance of a mail service. Ships sailing between London and the more established British colony of Jamaica would drop off a mail packet at Crooked Island in the south-central Bahamas, for further transport to Nassau. For out-islanders, mail could languish in Nassau for some time. It would eventually show up, but not on any dependable schedule. This comparative isolation was an economic roadblock as Bahamians never had a good sense of their markets for produce in Nassau and the United States. They had pineapples, sisal, sponges, lobsters and conch to sell, but were renowned for doing the wrong commercial thing at the wrong time. Produce often rotted before reaching market.

Bahamian Interlude - Pirates of The Bahamas

"Two bits, four bits, six bits, a dollar. All for the Pirates stand up and holler!!!!" A common chant you might expect to hear at a high school football game and it's certainly appropriate. But, two bits didn't come from a US dollar. It is much older than that and, although still

25

heard today, it's hardly relative in today's coinage that includes not only quarters, but also dimes, nickels and pennies.

The big colonial powers pretty much ignored the Bahamas, concentrating instead on other parts of the Caribbean, like Cuba and Hispaniola. The island group was uninhabited well into the 17th Century. However, one element appreciated the islands early in its modern history. Pirates loved it there! They knew the territory: shoals, sandbars, big underwater rocks, all the places where a collision calamity could happen to the unwary mariner. Here pirates could hide! In the early 1700s, the British awarded the islands to a group of "proprietors," private citizens given the right to govern the colony. They didn't do much with the mandate and a power vacuum prevailed. The Bahamian Islands were nearly ideal, first for privateers and later for pirates, to prey on Spanish shiploads of silver mined in the Americas and sent to Spain. With no real government control in the region, upwards of 1000 pirates occupied the Bahamas by 1713.

The "pirate era" started when the "privateer era" ended. In the early 1700s, England was at war with Spain and France. In Europe the war was about the Spanish succession, but in the New World the conflict centered on control over Florida between England and Spain, and over Canada between England and France. Wishing to disrupt the flow of silver to Spain and lacking the navy to do it themselves, England issued "letters of marque" or permits for private ships to attack Spanish and French ships during the war. "Privateering" was a swashbuckling, adventurous and lucrative life and it was great while it lasted. The Treaty of Utrecht between the waring powers ended the fun in 1715. Unwilling to give up the life and its rewards, privateers, stripped of their legal cover, became pirates, attacking ships of any nationality. Benjamin Hornigold in Eleuthera and Charles Vane in Abaco and many others were very successful for awhile, but the era was short lived. England regained control through the appointment in 1718 of former privateer Woods Rogers as governor of The Bahamas. Rogers and several British warships quickly restored order and the pirate era was over. Hornigold, once a mentor to Blackbeard, accepted a pardon and went on to other adventures, including tracking down and delivering several hold-out pirates to Rogers. Charles Vane, a pirate to the end, was hanged in 1721. Some pirates were more fortunate, and took their ill-gotten riches and went on to changed lives. Rogers, for his part, fared little better than the pirates he captured. Never supported adequately by either the proprietors or the crown, he turned to paying the colony's bills using his own fortune and by credit. After returning to London in 1722, Rogers was badly in debt and spent time in debtors prison. Ruined financially and in poor health, Woods Rogers died in Nassau in 1732. The location of his grave has been lost.

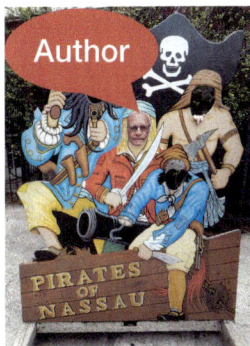

Pirates aplenty can still be found on the streets of Nassau. They are a little stiff!

Ok, then so what's with the "two bits?" Pieces of eight are historical Spanish coins minted in the Americas from the late 15th century through the 19th century. Made of silver, they were in nearly worldwide circulation by the late 19th century and were legal currency in the United States until 1857. The coin could be physically cut into eight pieces, or "bits," to make change — hence the colloquial name "pieces of eight," and "two bits" is a quarter.

Arrrgh! So how much does a pirate pay for corn-on-the-cob ?????
Buck-an-ear!!!!

The Emergence of Mailboats:

By 1821, the schooners Dash and Paragon were connecting islands within the Bahamas with mail coming from outside the colony. Any hope for economic development demanded more regular inter-island service, not just for mail, but also for passengers and cargo. The Bahamian government, urged by the

The 35 foot MailBoat Dart, provided service between Northern Eleuthera and Nassau. At just over fifty years, Dart was the longest-serving Bahamas mailboat until her replacement by a power vessel in 1920. The mailboat Captain Roberts had the opposite experience - wrecked on her maiden voyage in 1945 near Bimini.

islanders themselves, recognized that development in the Bahamas depended on improved and expanded "Inter-Insular Communications." In 1867, provisions were made to use fast sailing boats and extend service every two weeks from Nassau to communities in Eleuthera, Great Harbour Cay in the Berry Islands, and Cherokee and Green Turtle Cay in Abaco. By the mid-1880s, nearly 20 mailboats were serving 14 Bahamian communities in Central and Southern Bahamas.

The Modern Mailboat Era:

An "Act to Establish an Improved Inter-Insular Mail Service" was passed in 1948. The act empowered the Governor to establish mailboat contracts with private ship owners for service between Nassau and the Out-Islands, greatly expanding service to more communities. It also called for operational subsidies to ensure service to less profitable routes. The "Inter-Insular Mail

The MailBoat Bahamas Daybreak serves the small community of Governor's Harbour, Eleuthera.

Shipping Act of 1966," based on the 1948 act and the basis of legislation since, established fees standardized the carriage of mail, passengers and cargo within The Bahamas. The mailboat program is still in place today, the last legislation update coming in 2015. Today's fleet of mailboats serves over fifty communities on twenty Bahamian islands.

Chapter 3: Historic Mailboats

Author, maritime historian and mailboat traveler Eric Wiberg has counted and cataloged nearly 400 vessels that have provided mailboat services to the Bahama Islands over the past two-hundred years. Many were unique boats with colorful histories and had different origins. Some were wooden vessels constructed of native materials in the islands they served. Many, particularly in the mailboat beginning, had prior service lives. Some were converted yachts, providing a level of comfort for passengers not necessarily true of mailboats in general, but also not the best equipped to carry cargo. Others were discarded military vessels that were no longer needed in numbers following world wars. One or two of these boats even had a captured enemy submarine to their credit, before retiring to cart mail, cargo and passengers around the islands. One was a converted lifeboat, a picturesque craft and a survivor of a vessel that wrecked on a Bahamian reef. Some met maritime disaster during their mail service, ending their days on a rocky shore or in a watery grave. Many went on to other service after being relieved of their mail duties. Some of these had a gradual and graceful decline and often became the raw material for a new craft. Others found a more spectacular end in remote corners of the world. The following pages sample a few of these historical mailboats and tell their stories.

Albertine Adoue:

The *Albertine Adoue* was actually two boats. The first was a one hundred and seventy-foot, three-masted schooner built in Maine in 1890. She was wrecked three years later on a reef near Spanish Cay in the north-central Abaco Islands. Enterprising locals were always

***Albertine Adoue at Hope Town wharf on Elbow Cay,
Abaco Islands.*** *(Painting by Randy Curry of Green Turtle Cay,
Abaco, Bahamas, from a sketch by Laurie Jones. Randy's
Uncle Travis served on a successor Abaco MailBoat,
M/V Stede Bonnet.)*

on the lookout for "new boat building materials" showing up on area reefs, and the Albertine's timbers were quickly carted ashore to the boat-building center at Green Turtle Cay. *Albertine Adoue* soon re-emerged as a sixty-foot schooner. She served as MailBoat for the Abaco Islands for the next twenty-nine years.

By the early 1920s and in spite of her three decades of service, the *Albertine Adoue* fell out of favor with the Bahamian government:

"It is impossible in these progressive days," one Commissioner wrote in 1922, *"to expect a mail service to be satisfactorily performed by a sailing vessel."*

The *Albertine Adoue* was replaced as Abaco's MailBoat by the power vessel *Priscilla* in 1923. She was the last sailing vessel to serve Abaco as a mailboat, although the sloop *Arena* continued to haul cargo around the islands for another twenty-five years.

Captain Hartley Roberts was the last captain of the Albertine Adoue and the first captain of the Priscilla. He is honored in the Memorial Sculpture Garden, New Plymouth, Green Turtle Cay. His home can still be seen on Main Street.

Though *Priscilla* reduced Abaco's isolation and improved commerce, a colorful era in Bahamian history was ended. *Albertine Adoue* went on to other adventures and eventually met the same fate of her namesake predecessor. She was wrecked on the Outer Banks of

North Carolina while sneaking a boatload of rum into the United States during Prohibition.

Captain Dean:

In 1949, Ernest Dean hand-built the forty-foot, sloop-rigged auxiliary *Captain Dean* in Sandy Point on Great Abaco Island. Dean found his materials in the forests surrounding his Sandy Point home. After a long search, he found the ideal keel tree and dragged it through the forest to the beach and then towed it home behind his small sailing dinghy. Over the following year, he did the same for the frames, ribs and decking, searching the forest for just the right wood for the intended application. He took the next year to finish the boat in his beachside "shipyard."

When *Captain Dean* was ready, Dean contracted with the Bahamian government for mailboat services between Sandy Point, Abaco and Nassau. He eventually added more locations to his route. The *Captain Dean* served as a mailboat for years, but was eventually sold to acquire funds to pay for the construction of *Captain Dean III*. Decades later, Ernest Dean, then nearly 80, while looking to buy a couple of groupers for dinner, came upon an aging boat along the docks in Nassau where the fishing boats tied up. She was painted all white, her mast and long boom had been removed, her graceful bowsprit had been replaced by a short stubby one, and the one time beauty was gone. But, she was the *Captain Dean* and still operating and continued into the early 1990s. Her eventual fate is unknown. *Captain Dean* started a family mailboat dynasty that continues today.

The Captain Dean, first of many Dean family MailBoats
*(Painting by Randy Curry. Original model
photo provided by the Dean family)*

City of Nassau:

During the wooden-boat-sail era, Bahamians mostly built their own boats for the mail service. That changed during the sail to power transition and, for a time, a primary source of mailboats for the Bahamas was old freighters purchased from Europe. One such purchase was the *SS Laura,* a large coal-fired steamship built in Scotland in 1885. She had provided trade service in the Channel Islands. *Laura* was renamed the *City of Nassau* in 1927 by her new Bahamian owners upon her arrival in her new country.

City of Nassau departing Nassau Harbour passing the lighthouse. *(Painting by Randy Curry. Randy's Godparents, Noel and Ivy Roberts, were the keepers of the Nassau lighthouse for many years.)*

Coal-fired, *City of Nassau* posed immediate problems as the Bahamas lacked coaling stations.

Additionally, anyone who has cruised in the Bahama Islands knows that her 13-foot draft would not do well in many locations. As a result of her limitations, she served mostly between Harbour Island, Eleuthera and Nassau, an active route to this day and one where deep water could be found throughout. She also sailed between Miami and Nassau.

Eventually, European cast-offs were eliminated, and steel power vessels were built specifically for the mailboat trade with a draft and configuration suitable to the Bahamas. Eric Wiberg reports that the *City of Nassau's* fate is murky – she was either broken up for scrap or lost during bootlegging. Another source has her lasting in some capacity until 1957.

Air Swift:

Former military boats were also popular as mailboats for a time. Built of wood in 1943 in Long Island, New York, *Air Swift* began life as *USS SC 1340*, a WW II era SC-497 Class Submarine Chaser. Nothing much is recorded about her service, but she must have

WW II era SC-497 Class Submarine Chaser. Similar to Air Swift in military mode. *(Public domain photo)*

37

found some use for her 40mm gun mount, two .50 caliber machine guns, two depth charge projector "Y Guns," and two depth charge tracks! Following the war, she became *USCGC WAVR 471 Air Swift* for a few years. As in her submarine chaser days, her USCG service is equally fuzzy. While her military service seems nondescript, following her purchase in 1948 for the mailboat trade, *Air Swift* became the well-known mainstay on the Spanish Wells to Nassau route for the next twenty-five years. She was replaced eventually by the *Bahamas Daybreak*, a mailboat of today.

Air Swift as MailBoat passing through Spanish Wells, Eleuthera. *(Painting by Randy Curry. Randy's Spanish Wells relatives remember Air Swift well and provided details for the painting. Original model photo courtesy of Dave Gayle of Abaco, Bahamas.)*

Like many mailboats, *Air Swift* went on to other service. Eric Wiberg reports that in the 1970s the ship's

New York builder was attracted to an aging freighter while on vacation in the Bahamas. He verified her identity by scraping away at an old metal placard buried in a hull location only the builder would know about. *Air Swift* met her eventual demise by being beaten to death against a rock in Nassau Harbour where she sank. She was later cut up and destroyed by the Bahamian government. It was a sad and dubious end to a great and historic boat.

Chapter 4: Mailboat Travel 101

Today, just under seventy percent of all Bahamians live in Nassau, the country's capital and commercial center. Nassau grew in favor over the earlier settled Eleuthera due to its excellent harbor and proximity to the deep-water ocean passes that separate the Great and Little Bahama Banks with Florida and Cuba. Originally founded in 1670 as Charles Town, it was burned to the ground by the Spanish, rebuilt and renamed Nassau in 1685. Sparsely settled and with no resident English governor, the area became a pirate haven into the early-1700s, with notable residents Charles Vane, Calico Jack Rackham, Anne Bonny, Mary Read and the infamous Edward Teach, better known as "Blackbeard."

A new English governor regained control of Nassau after 1718 and the area grew modestly. Nassau's modern growth began in the late eighteenth century, with the influx of thousands of American Loyalists and their slaves into the Bahamas following the American War of Independence. Since World War II, the entire island of New Providence on which Nassau sits, has continued to grow in population and commercial importance.

Potters Cay - Mailboat Heaven:

With the city's commercial dominance, Nassau would emerge as the "hub" of the mailboat system and the routes to the Family (Out) Islands, the "spokes." Most visitors, especially those arriving by cruise ship, see little more of the country than Nassau and the nearby resort center of Paradise Island (previously Hog Island before the resorts were built!) Unsuspecting travelers have no idea that the gateway to the Family Islands and the *real Bahamas*, lies on a small, busy, little cay under the two high-rise bridge spans that connect Nassau proper with Paradise Island and the mega-resorts located there. Few places on Earth are as chaotic as Potters Cay. With the up-scale Atlantis mega-resort looming in the background on nearby Paradise Island, Potters is a beehive of shipping activity whose seemingly disorganized choreography is a marvel to watch. Mailboat travelers spend a lot of enjoyable time doing just that!

Dave Blake Photography

Potters Cay viewed from the Sidney Poitier Bridge connecting Nassau and Paradise Island.

Boats of all descriptions are loaded on Potters Cay.

The Mailboat Fleet:

By today's count, eighteen vessels operate with the moniker *mail vessel*. Most of the current boats are about the size of *Captain Gurth Dean,* pictured in the Forward. They are officially sanctioned and subsidized to carry mail, and by extension, cargo and passengers throughout the islands. Mailboats depart from Potters Cay in Nassau and generally visit several small communities on one or two islands, returning to Nassau in a few days or close to a week later. They repeat the process the following week. Also available for transport are a number of "Bahamas Ferries," larger vessels with "roll-on roll-off" capabilities for ease with cargo, but also carry many passengers. The big boats cover fewer destinations, but sail more often and have set schedules. Other ferries are configured primarily for passengers, but also carry a lot of cargo. They all carry mail. Though not all boats are designated mail vessels, to the traveler they all do the same things and are available to explore the many corners of a terrific and most interesting country. In some island groups, people ferries and water taxis provide close-in,

Dave Blake Photography

inter-island transfers. You can go anywhere in The Bahamas by boat!

Dave Blake Photography

Bahamas couldn't function without boats! Roll-on-roll-off vessels and smaller mailboats provide most of the heavy lifting. People (and mail) ride on both. Many Bahamians live on one island and work on another. The smaller ferries and people movers operate all day and also carry cargo - whatever you can lug aboard!

Mailboat Travel:

Mailboat travel offers an extraordinary opportunity to see a part of this wonderful world as it is. Whether it is a mode of travel for you will, hopefully, be answered in the coming chapters as you read through actual "mailboat adventures." Mailboat travel requires an adventurous spirit, an appreciation for communities that are not necessarily on a top ten travel list, flexibility, a tolerance for accommodations, and an acceptance of some uncertainty in your eventual destination and accommodations once you arrive.

Here are a few details on how it all works:

* Mailboat schedules are published and are easily accessible on line. However, schedules change often

and need to be checked close to a travel date. Even with recent information, schedules might still change. On the next page is a sample schedule. Helpful search items for planning are listed in Chapter 13.

* Your initial departure will be from Potters Cay. Plan on a day or two in Nassau in advance of planned travel to walk the docks and talk to crews. The best information will come from the crews themselves. Even then, you can't be sure.

* It is best to have a variety of possible destinations when planning a trip. Your first choice may not depart as planned, leaving you homeless. Having alternative choices enhances your chances of leaving on the day you planned.

* For most mail vessel designated boats, tickets are purchased onboard. The Bahamas Ferries and the big MailBoat (cover photo) and a few others have ticket booths on Potters Cay and tickets can be purchased in advance for predictable sailing dates in the near term.

* It is true that you can get almost anywhere in the Bahamas by boat. Getting back, however, is not always so easy! Except in Nassau, mailboats rarely spend more than a few hours at any stop, making it impossible to arrive at an island, spend a day or two to see the sights and then proceed on to another destination. Unless you want to wait where you end up until the next week's mailboat for a return, alternate transportation needs to be considered. If you are lucky (emphasis on lucky), you can hitch a ride to a nearby island and later catch a mailboat back to Nassau from there.

* If you get stuck, you can almost always fly to Nassau to get back on track. Bahamas Air goes everywhere in the Bahamas and ALWAYS to Nassau. Inter-island air transportation is inexpensive.

MAILBOAT SCHEDULE (TYPICAL)

Mailboat/Fare	Destination	Nassau Departure	Return	Length of Trip
Bahamas Daybreak III $30	Eleuthera Rock Sound Davis Harbour Harbour Island	Mondays 5:00 p.m. Wednesdays 6.00 p.m.	Tuesdays 8:00 p.m. Sundays 3:00 p.m.	5 hrs
Bimini Mack $45	North Bimini. Alice Town Cat Cay	Thursdays	Mondays	12 hrs
Grand Master $40	Exuma Georgetown	Tuesdays	Fridays	12 hrs
Mal Jack $35	South Andros Mangrove Cay Kemps Bay Bluff	Mondays 10 p.m. Fridays 10 p.m.	Wednesdays 10 p.m. Sundays 10 p.m.	6 hrs
Lady Eddina $40	Cat Island Bennett Hbr	Thursdays 6 p.m.	Sundays 2 p.m.	14 hrs

Note: MailBoat schedules are easily researched on-line, but change frequently. The above schedule is offered as an illustration. Mailboats operate throughout The Bahamas. Additional information on schedules is provided in Appendix B.

Nassau Harbour: Paradise Island is on the left and Nassau proper on the right. The two Islands are connected by the Sidney Poitier Bridge. Potters Cay is the small island under the double-span bridge at the top of the photo.

Once armed with a schedule, mailboat travel axioms apply: Stay flexible, laugh a lot and take many photos to send home to disbelieving friends and family. Above all, enjoy the "real Bahamas" you will visit and the "real Bahamians" you will meet. In the following chapters, a few adventures are described and highlight this writer's continuing fascination with mailboat travel. Decide for yourself if it's for you!

Chapter 5: MailBoat I
The First Adventure

During the past several years, a group of friends traveled to many Bahamian islands and visited dozens of communities, mostly by mailboat with an occasional airplane thrown into the mix. Although occasionally ending up in an unanticipated location with uncertain digs upon arrival, we escaped sleeping on a beach even once, though we were prepared for the possibility. Here are our tales.

Nassau and New Providence:

Having finally decided to try mailboat travel in 2017, I convinced two old college friends to try it with me. A few weeks later, Dave Blake arrived from Arizona and Phil Lugger arrived from Michigan, and we all met in Nassau to begin our adventure. Arriving on a Friday, we had a few days to prepare for our first planned destination. Kemps Bay on South Andros Island was our first choice, a seven-hour trip for $30 aboard *M/V Moxey.* After getting a rental car and finding a hotel, our first act was to check out Potters Cay and investigate how we might get tickets. *Moxey* wasn't departing for South Andros Island until Monday. We located the berthing spot where *Moxey* would dock upon her return on Sunday. People on the dock indicated we would just buy tickets on board before departure, scheduled for 11 pm. Satisfied that we had a plan for Monday's departure, we set out to explore our immediate surroundings.

Armed with a couple of days to spare and a rental car, we headed across the island to where I had visited in my Catalina 30 *Rhombus* during a 2012 sail. Although considerably more up-scale than many other places we would visit, New Providence outside of Nassau is a delightful Bahamian island worthy of exploration. We happened upon a tiny port called Stuart Cove, home of a dive and snorkel tour company that also offered underwater tours in tiny *yellow submarines!* With the drumbeat of the Beatles' song in our heads, how could three "children of the 60s" resist? We made reservations for the next day's ride and continued our auto tour of the island. We returned to Stuart Cove the next day for our scheduled rides in the tiny vessels. The little boats are ridden like a motorcycle with a small electric motor and air forced into an open-to-the water head bubble to allow for normal breathing. We donned wet suits, climbed into our little yellow boats, and descended to a maximum of twenty feet, a depth maintained by a tether attached to a float.

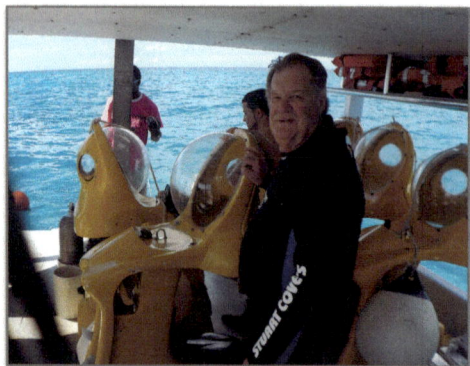

Dave gets ready for the "under voyage."

We were in the first of two groups and I was given the honor of handling the fish food used to attract some underwater life. We were already surrounded by hundreds of colored fish, which evidently knew the routine. Unfortunately, when I let loose of the sumptuous feast, some of it floated up inside my bubble, soon visited by several yellow-tail fish anxious for a meal. I couldn't get them to leave my bubble! Unknown to me, I had received several dorsal fin inflicted lacerations and blood was streaming down my

"We all live in a yellow submarine, yellow submarine, yellow submarine!!!" (Fred left, Dave center, Phil right)

© Phil Lugger

face as I surfaced twenty minutes later. Needless-to-say, I made a BIG impression on the second group of submariners waiting for their turn!

My Submarine, before and after fish food!!!

© Phil Lugger

49

Long Island:

After a great weekend, we returned to Potters Cay to catch the *M/V Moxey's* Monday departure to South Andros Island. In doing so we discovered mailboat travel rule one:

"Written mailboat schedules are approximate."

Moxey wouldn't leave until Tuesday! Homeless, we looked for alternatives and had two: relatively near-by Georgetown in the Exumas and Long Island, way down south. We opted for Long Island aboard the *Sea Wind* captained by, you might guess, Captain Moxey, a nephew. The mailboat world, it seems, is a family affair. More about that later.

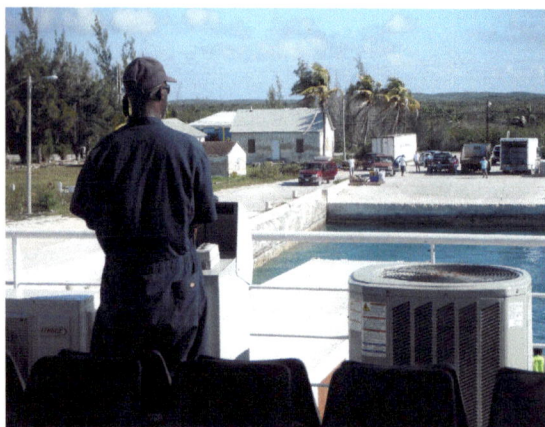

Captain Moxey guides the Sea Wind into Simms, Long Island.

Dave and Phil, my two companions and fraternity brothers for a half century, suffered a bit on the 19 hour open ocean voyage to Long Island. I slept like a baby - an advantage of a quarter century in the US Navy and a lifetime of small boat cruising. We arrived in the early morning and found a glorious rural Bahamian Island. We were met by Bernard at the ferry dock, our ride to the Winter Haven Hotel in Clarence Town. The hotel is a family run beach jewel with about eight rooms, the Rowdy Boys Bar and Grill and friendly people.

Long Island's rocky side shoreline.

We loved it and we began to explore the island. You can hike many of the Out-islands, but not this one. Barely a mile wide in many spots, we rented a car to tour this 80 mile-long island, split by the Tropic of Cancer in its northern third. You don't need a map, there is only one 80 mile-long road! The island is noted for its varied topography, dramatic cliffs and caves on the east coast and broad sandy beaches on the lee west side, fitting the geological model of the Bahamas formation. Our island hikes and excursions took on a differing character depending on terrain. It is beautiful everywhere!

The biggest Long Island hit was Dean's Blue Hole, where the aquamarine water of the near shore

Always a photographer Dave waits for the perfect shot to capture Long Island's beauty and there is a lot of it to capture!!

Our Long Island stay, the Winter Haven Hotel in Clarence Town.

Dave Blake Photography

gives way at its center to the deep blue color of the open ocean. It's the world's second deepest blue hole, plunging almost 700 feet with circular stone walls to the ocean floor. Noted as the world's best place for free dives, the current "Free Immersion Dive" record (wetsuit and no fins) tops 400 feet. The "Ultra-Free Immersion Dive" record (no fins or wetsuit or any suit - sometimes called "skinny dipping,") was established during our visit! If you venture to Long Island, think about climbing into the record books. The free dive record is out of reach, but the "ultra-free" dive record stands at a little over ten feet!

An unidentified visitor tries and sets the "Ultra-Free Immersion Dive" Record at Dean's Blue Hole on the Southeastern shore of Long Island, Bahamas!

As much as we loved Long Island, we only had two weeks and wanted to see more. Our target was near-by San Salvador, a little to the northeast and historically significant as Columbus' first landing spot in the New World. However, we found it much easier getting to Long Island than leaving it. With no mailboat on the horizon and having exhausted other marine transport possibilities, we turned to Freddy!

Bahamian Interlude - Ocean Blue Holes

Blue holes are unknown to most of us, but are spectacular when we first see them. Roughly circular, steep-walled ocean depressions, they are so named for the dramatic contrast between the dark blue, deep waters of the hole and the lighter blue of the shallows that surround them. Blue holes are large marine caverns which are open to the surface and have developed in a bank or island composed of a carbonate bedrock of

The Great Blue Hole in Belize

limestone or in a coral reef. They formed during past ice ages, when the sea level was much lower than at present. Simply stated, on the banks of a blue hole you can step from a sandy shore into hundreds of feet of water! Spectacular they are!!

The visually most attractive blue hole is almost certainly the Great Blue Hole, located near Ambergris Caye, Belize. The deepest blue hole was for decades thought to be Dean's Blue Hole in Long Island, Bahamas. However, the Dragon Hole in the South China Sea was measured at just under a thousand feet, a third deeper than Dean's depth. Interestingly, most of the rest of the world's blue holes are less than half the depth of these two. While the Bahamas no longer claims the deepest blue hole, it has a mother lode of them. Dozens are scattered throughout the country, particularly on Andros Island where more than 50 are recorded. Many *are in The Blue Holes National Park.*

Located on an ocean beach with easy access to Clarence Town, Long Island's "Dean's Blue Hole" is a popular attraction. The site received added attention in 2008 when New Zealander William Trubridge announced that a major diving competition called Vertical Blue would be held at the site. A star-studded cast of the world's top free divers would compete. Termed the "Clash of the Titans," Trubridge personally put up the $20,000 prize money, then quickly won and took it home with him. He repeated the feat for several years until an Austrian competitor pocketed his money. The Vertical Blue competition continues to be held annually. The men's record tops 400 feet, the women's 300 feet. The "Ultra-Free Immersion" record is still around ten feet, as far as I know!

San Salvador:

Intending to go to San Salvador following Long Island, we had discussed possible transport with the crew of the MailBoat that traveled between the two islands while still in Potters Cay. But the boat didn't sail that week, introducing mailboat travel rule two:

"You can't find out where and when mailboats are really going without talking to the crew, and even then you can't be sure!"

After unsuccessfully trying to entice fishermen and other boat owners for a ride, we settled on Freddy. He picked us up on the north end of Long Island, after we got a ride from Clarence Town in the south. With no regular commercial land transportation, Dawn Simmons, Executive of the Long Island Tourist Office, delivered us to Freddy, a hundred miles out of her way on the way to work! It was just one example of the extraordinary service we received from The Bahamas Tourist Bureaus during our travels. Freddy swooped in from the north, and we were soon on our way.

Dave Blake Photography

Freddie Air lands on a north Long Island air strip to pick us up.

It was a five-seater, but Phil takes up a couple of them and for weight and balance, I was awarded the right seat. Twenty minutes after our departure from Long Island, we arrived in the more upscale tourist center of San Salvador to begin another adventure. Disappointed that our boat trip would turn to aviation for a ride, we were happy to get to an island with a little more activity, illustrating mailboat travel rule three:

"Alternate transportation sometimes needs to be considered."

San Salvador also had historical interest as the first foreign Bahamas cruiser paid a visit here on

October 12,1492. Later in our visit, we would spend half a day hiking to the Christopher Columbus monument!

Freddy landed in Cockburn Town, which unlike Long Island, actually has stores, restaurants and bars. There would be less beach exploration on this visit! It didn't take us long to find a favorite, local-color watering hole. Wendy's was across from the little airport. For accommodations, our habit was to contact the local tourist office and provide our standard criteria for a hotel, simple but nice. They got it right every time and we soon found ourselves at the delightful Sands Hotel. A more guide-book prominent hotel was next door, but Jermaine Johnson, Senior Executive at the Tourist Office, recommended the Sands. How right he was! We checked into our terrific little beach hotel, a family-owned place still recovering from the affects of the 2005 Hurricane Joaquin, as were most of the islands of the Central Bahamas.

Once settled, we made plans for our two full days of island exploration yet to come. Arrival day was time to relax and enjoy our pleasant surroundings. Kerry Ann, the hotel office manager, took us to the store for some needed "groceries." We also met her delightful daughter Denise, who tagged along. Denise let it be known that she really liked skittles, and she got a bag every day of our stay. When we inquired about renting a car to explore the island, the Sands' Hilton Ferguson offered to loan us the hotel car for the next day, "just buy a little gas." He also let us use it after the hotel office closed in the evenings. Service with a smile!

With our borrowed wheels, we started our grand tour by circumnavigating the island, a trip of about fifty miles. San Salvador is half the area and with 940

Dave Blake Photography

Dave Blake Photography

Sands Hotel, Cockburn Town, San Salvador. "Sweet Denise" lit up our stay!

residents, has a third of the population of the much larger Long Island, but with a considerable up-tick in terms of activity. Sampling all the island's sights, we often returned to Wendy's to enjoy a cold beer and a multitude of colorful characters. High on our list of must-do's was the Columbus Monument, positioned on top of the island's highest hill. It wasn't easy to get to. The first part of the trip was up and down and up a boulder and rock-strewn auto path that allowed only idle speed. Mindful that we were in a borrowed car, we went even slower and eventually arrived at a spot where climbing by foot was required. We weren't the youngest group at the top! We celebrated the moment like three Everest explorers, enjoyed the view from San Salvador's

"I don't think Columbus ever climbed up here!"

The view on the way down from the monument was spectacular, inviting a swim at the end!

rooftop, then started our way back down. Unfortunately, we forgot the champagne!

Most of the tourist traffic to San Salvador is headed to the Club Med Resort called "Columbus Isle." The club doesn't admit day-trippers, but Jermaine Johnson, the local tourist office head, again came to our rescue. "I have three gentlemen doing work for the Tourist Ministry," I overheard him say over the phone after telling him I would write about our travels. Our day at Columbus Isle was set and we three septuagenarians looked forward to another brand of *"flora and fauna!*

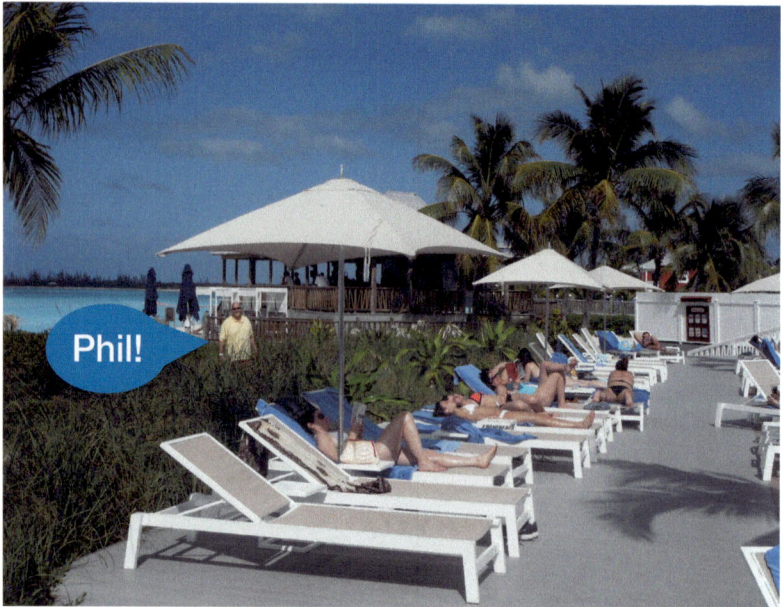

Columbus Isle is an all-inclusive resort and we enjoyed a full day of conspicuous consumption, while spending time in the pool, enjoying beach toys, and passing by the outdoor bar once or twice. We also took a little time out for a little photography! Hungry a couple of hours after our arrival, we headed for lunch. The

We enjoyed all things beautiful at Club Med San Salvador.

lunch buffet was 125 feet long, plus another fifteen feet or so of wine table! Our day's visa expired at Sundown, good thing! Luckily also, the resort was a short distance from the Sands Hotel. Thanks Bahamas Tourist Bureau!!!

Bahamian Interlude - The First Bahamas Cruiser

Well, Columbus wasn't exactly the first, but he was certainly the most celebrated. The Antilleans, Arawaks, and Taino all beat him to the mark and the Lucayans greeted him upon arrival. Exactly where they welcomed him ashore is still debated.

Christoforo Colombo, to use his Italian name, was born in Genoa in 1451 to a middle-class family. Though

61

encouraged to enter business, he dreamed of going to sea. Marrying into a Portuguese seafaring family, Columbus got his wish and became a trader to West Africa and around the Mediterranean. He also did time as a mapmaker. There were a lot of holes in his maps and he hoped to fill in the blanks. He conjured up a bold plan to establish a new trade route to "Cathay." By going directly west across the "Western Ocean," he would avoid using the Silk Road land route or the known hazardous sea route around the Horn of Africa. Like other ocean sailors of the day, Columbus was under no delusions that the Earth wasn't a sphere and he theorized that China lay only 5000 miles west of the Canary Islands.

Needing massive financial backing to put his idea into action, Columbus shopped his plan among the capitals of Europe. He finally got the help he needed from Queen Isabella of Spain. Newly appointed as Admiral of the Ocean Sea, Columbus set sail on August 2, 1492 with three ships. The Nina, Pinta and Santa Maria are ship names well known by school kids today. The voyage itself is well chronicled. Columbus kept a detailed log and made copious notes, which played a role later in determining on exactly which island he first landed. Columbus' own notes report that they were warmly greeted. The Lucayans believed they would one day be visited by strange voyagers from the vast Eastern Ocean, "who must certainly be gods."

Columbus himself made benevolent descriptions of the gentle people he had found. Both he and they had entered a 'new world' and neither imagined the human disaster that lay ahead. Columbus would play a major role in what would happen to these gentle people during later voyages to the Caribbean.

An excerpt from Columbus' log is attributed to the Lucayans plus a painting depicting the scene:

"Come and see the men who have arrived from Heaven; bring them food and drink."

 Centuries later, a debate arose over which Bahama Island is the site of the initial landfall. Bahamian historical tradition cited Cat Island, then given the Columbus name of San Salvador. Considerable study of Columbus' logs and his descriptions of his surroundings made while underway later identified Watlings Island, a little to the southeast of Cat Island, as the probable landing site. On May 6, 1926, San Salvador was renamed Cat Island and Watlings Island became San Salvador. Yet, even today, not everyone is convinced. One interesting historical note is pointed out by Peter Barrett in his book, Bahama Saga, from which much of this article is taken:

 "It is interesting, almost ironic, to recall that Columbus, in being the first European to find the 'new world' by his landfall in the Bahamas, actually found the last land to be discovered by the original Asian explorers."

63

While a case can be made for other locations for that first Columbus landfall, I'm throwing in my lot with San Salvador. I'd hate to think I climbed that mountain for nothing!

Chapter 6: Eleuthera
Harbour Island and Spanish Wells

San Salvador was terrific, but it was time to go. We visited Wendy's Bar one last time, spent a quiet night at the hotel, and prepared for our return to Nassau the next day. We had long boat rides ahead of us and more islands to explore. Once again we would find ourselves in new surroundings, never certain beforehand exactly where that would be. Returning to Nassau, Dave, Phil and I only had a week to explore the remaining three islands on our "hope to visit" list. We also had to get back to Nassau one final time to catch our scheduled flights home. Luckily, all three islands on our list are part of Eleuthera, are in close proximity to each other, and have frequent boat transportation from Nassau to Eleuthera and between the islands. We've had a wonderful time, but there were island experiences yet to come!

Current, Eleuthera:

Our timing was perfect. We arrived at Potters Cay mid-day on a Sunday, just in time to catch the Sea Link to the little town of Current on the Northwestern tip of Eleuthera. We waited a couple of hours for *Sea Link* to finish loading as we enjoyed the sights and sounds of always exciting Potters Cay. The sea cruise was highlighted by the sundown appearance of the famous "green flash," the instantaneous flash of bright green light that rarely follows the last gasp of daylight, as Ole Sol dips below the horizon. I've watched for green flashes during a lifetime of sea travel and have seen only three. Phil and Dave saw their first green flash only seconds after they learned what they are!

Dave Blake Photography

Sea Link loads cargo, mail and passengers. Sunset on the Sea Link as we cruised toward Current Island. We were soon treated to a rare "green flash," a green beam of light either shooting up or seen just after "Ole Sol" dips below the horizon.

A late afternoon departure got us to Eleuthera Sunday evening. I'd been to Current before, or at least sailed by it during previous sailing trips. Nearby is Current Cut, between Current Island and mainland Eleuthera. It is narrow and has a maximum tidal current of 10 knots. Five-knot boats must take notice of 10 knot currents and I approached it then with great trepidation! Though I watched carefully, *Sea Link* sped through the cut with no apparent concern. By late Sunday evening, we were deposited ashore in the tiny and very-quiet town of Current. It was a Sunday night in a little town that's quiet on any night and if ever we were going to spend a night on the beach, this was it. Mailboat travel rule four:

"You won't always know where you'll sleep when you get there, but you'll find a place."

Cab driver Foster met us at the mailboat landing, and learning that we were homeless offered; "No problem, I'll take you over to Jeans!" In the small nearby town of Bluff, Eleuthera, Jean Newry and her family took us in with open arms! The family had built a couple of

66

rooms in a garden behind their house and named the complex "EarlDora," after their parents. Their hope was to occasionally snag a couple of tourists needing a place to stay after getting off the mailboat. We were perfect. Jean booted out a couple of family members currently staying in the rooms and moved them into their house. While Foster took us on a run to get some needed libations, Jean cleaned the rooms and they were ready when we returned. After a great breakfast with the family the next morning, Foster showed up to deliver us to the water taxi landing serving Harbour Island, our destination. What an unexpectedly delightful stay in the "Bluff." Mailboat travel has a way of working out that way.

Jean Newry and her family took great care of us!

Harbour Island:

Harbour Island and its Dunmore Town comprise a picture-perfect little seaside place. With mainland Eleuthera and nearby Spanish Wells, this compact area is hard to beat no matter how you get there. I had a wonderful time sailing through this area in 2012 and again in 2018, but if a MailBoat is your transportation choice and you have a schedule to keep, northern

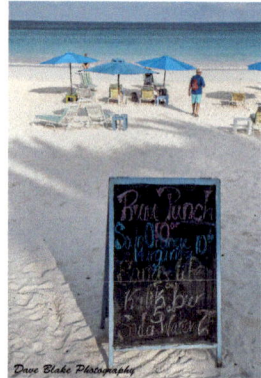

Harbour Island has a cute town, beautiful beaches, and an active restaurant row.

Eleuthera and its nearby islands offer the best and most frequent connections. Soon after Foster delivered us to the water taxi landing, we arrived at Harbour Island. We opted for the Hotel Royal near the center of Dunmore Town, giving us quick access to the harbor-side activity and the beautiful ocean beaches. We could easily walk it all, but rented a golf cart anyway. Harbour Island is definitely a tourist mecca and is easily the most upscale place we had visited. Having spent most of our trip in the very rural Bahamas, we were ready for the change. Picturesque Dunmore Town has it all for visitors. Restaurants and watering holes line the harbor-side, and boating facilities are in the center of activity. There are even stores, not always true in out-island Bahamian towns. We spent our days touring in our golf cart or at the ocean beach and the evenings listening to live music at the Queen Conch Inn. Our three days were over too soon!

Mainland Eleuthera:

In two previous trips to the area, my Catalina 30 Rhombus and I sailed the length of Eleuthera's 100 mile-long, main island, which sports a cute town and an inviting anchorage every twenty miles or so. Cruising in prevailing easterlies along the western lee shore of the narrow north-to-south oriented island, presented as pleasant a sailing experience as I've had in over forty years of active cruising and I wanted to share some of that time with my friends. So we rented a car for a day of exploration on the big island. High on my list to showcase were the Glass Window Bridge and Hatchet Bay. A few miles south of the island's northern tip, Eleuthera narrows at the Glass Window to the width of the highway. You can anchor on the Exuma Sound side and see the Atlantic Ocean under the highway bridge. Often called the "narrowest place on Earth," the bridge replaced a long arch destroyed during a hurricane. We stopped just short of the bridge to marvel at this bridge-wide island, and to take a few photos. The Atlantic side cliffs decorate Eleuthera's spectacular eastern shore, while the gentle-sloping western shoreline is also evident. It's an amazing topographical change in such a short distance and consistent with the geological development of the islands.

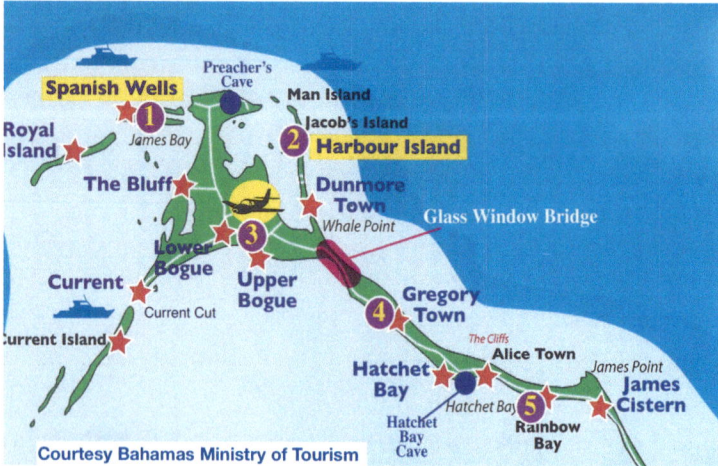

Photos taken from the Glass Window Bridge FROM THE SAME SPOT!! Left is the deep blue of the Atlantic Ocean and right the shallow aquamarine waters of Exuma Sound.

We then pressed on to my second must-revisit

site, Hatchet Bay, which occupies a special "white knuckle" place in my cruising memory. *Rhombus* and I had been anxious about the entry to Hatchet Bay. With nary a marine marker or even a stake in sight, we proceeded through the narrow opening after a lengthy period of surveillance and contemplation, hoping that the entrance was indeed the entrance and not just a shallow break in a large pile of rocks.

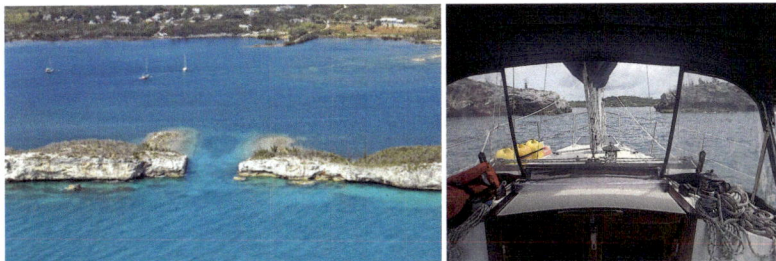

Hatchet Bay was an inland lake. An opening was blasted to make it a harbor. Rhombus' birds eye view of the entrance is from a 2012 sailing trip.

Navigating a rental car this time with Dave and Phil, it looked pretty easy. After visiting nearby Alice Town, we continued south to Governor's Harbour, for me another special cruising place. Governor's Harbour is likely the beginning site of the resettlement of the Bahamas after the departure of the original population. I had twice spent a few quiet days there at anchor during prior sailing trips. Following lunch, we headed back north for our last night on Harbour Island.

Spanish Wells:

We couldn't have enjoyed Harbour Island more, but it was time to move on. The town of Spanish Wells occupies all of the two-mile-long St. Georges Cay and is just off the northwestern corner of the main island, opposite Harbour Island on the northeastern corner. We had a choice of watercraft to get there, two water taxis separated by a cab ride, or the *Bo Hengy II*. We liked the looks of Bo and she offered the added treat of passing through the famed "Devil's Backbone," the shallow and jagged-edged reef that snakes its way around the northern end of Eleuthera between Harbour Island and Spanish Wells. Known as a snorkeler's paradise, the Backbone has plenty of water, as long as you can find it! Guides are recommended for private boats that transit the waterway, and I hired one for the short piece that I traveled through during sailing trips.

Bo Hengy II loads at Harbour Island Dock.

Charming Spanish Wells is what an active fishing village should look like. The fleet that calls Spanish Wells home fishes a wide swath of the Atlantic looking for their prime catch, spiny lobster, called crawfish by the Bahamians. After an exhilarating ride through the Devil's Backbone, we arrived at this picturesque town and were dropped right in front of the Vacation Time Suites hotel office, our planned stay for our last island. The actual hotel was on the harbor, several blocks away. Fortunately, the office also rented golf carts and within a few minutes of the Bo Hengy's arrival in port, we had our lodging and our wheels all arranged. Our two-bedroom suite with a kitchen was perfect - a block

Captain Fred on the Spanish Wells waterfront. A lobster boat is in the background.

from the bridge to Russell Island - just across the narrow waterway with a terrific little park and beach. We dumped our stuff and took our golf cart to get some "groceries" to stock our kitchen for our three-day visit. Our golf cart tours of the island frequently ended at Buddas or the Shipyard, our two favorite emporiums, lamenting the fact that this terrific trip was nearing its end. Spanish Wells has it all: great beaches, modest and attractive places to stay, and lively nightspots, all of it with the added treat of being in the center of a vibrant fishing community. Crews were busy working on their boats and rigs, but were happy to take a break to chat with interested visitors. Also, along the main dock in the center of town is the world's most compact boatyard, adding to the interesting activity of a very active small, picturesque town.

Dave Blake Photography

Dave Blake Photography

The Spanish Wells Harbor Front

Vacation Time Suites - our room in Spanish Wells

Each Bahamian town has its own charm, but none have more of it than Spanish Wells. The town is captivating at first look and, with a population of around 1500, is busier than most Bahamian towns. It has a decidedly middle-class feel: no resorts, no high-rise condos or mega-estates, only well-maintained homes, and everybody seems to have a job. Spanish Wells is a treasure, a place where strangers wave to each other and it's hard to just take a walk as people stop to pick you up. I'm sure the community has its troubles, but they're hard to spot. We loved it!

The *Bo Hengy II* is a rocket ship compared to most mailboats. We were back in Nassau in no time for one last night ashore before catching our flights home. We had visited eight islands in two weeks, including upscale tourist centers and the quietest small towns and rural communities where a hardware store, which also served breakfast and draft beer, was one of our favorite stops. We hiked a multitude of miles, walked leagues of beaches, collected a bushel of sea glass, and even set a diving record. Through it all, we saw a lot of the real Bahamas and scores of real Bahamians. We were hatching plans for MailBoat II before we again saw Nassau.

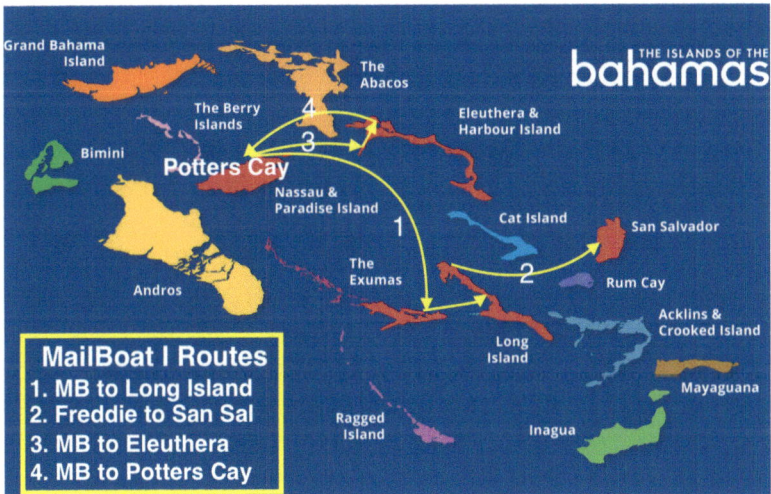

Eight islands down, six-hundred ninety-two to go!!!

Bahamian Interlude - "Spiny" Lobsters

The sloop or schooner-rigged Bahamian fishing smack is one of the classic boats of the region and Bahamians have long looked to the sea for both personal subsistence and commerce. Some marine animals, like sea turtles and sponges, have come and gone as important food sources or commercial exports. While the declining numbers of turtles and the advent of synthetic sponges curtailed their importance in Bahamian life, one marine animal has for generations continued to fulfill both needs - the Caribbean Spiny Lobster. Bahamians call them crawfish. One very big American restaurant chain and seller of the animal uses the "lobster" name. It seems that "Red Crawfish" doesn't have a nice marketing ring! Superficially, spiny lobsters resemble Maine lobsters in terms of overall shape and having a hard carapace and exoskeleton. However, they can easily be distinguished by very long, thick, spiny antennae, and by the lack of claws characteristic of their northern relatives.

Spiny lobsters are very interesting critters. They prefer to live in crevices of rocks and coral reefs, and venture out at night to seek snails, clams, sea hares, sea urchins and other tasty delectables. They are great smellers and can map the ocean floor to locate food by flashing their long antennae through the water. They navigate using both the smell and taste of natural substances in the water that change in different parts of the ocean. They also get around by detecting the Earth's magnetic field. One factoid popular with kids is that these animals are not only fast-a-foot, they flap their tails to swim backwards and are faster than a dolphin! Their long survival and large population might be explained by their camouflage coloring, sharp spines that can cut (as *this author can attest through personal experience) and they can really scoot! Spiny Lobsters have been swimming the Caribbean for a long time. Their fossil record dates back 110 million years.*

Lobsters have been hunted in the Bahamas for a millennium before there were modern Bahamians. In modern times they were fished from a dinghy or a small fishing boat. Two men with long poles, a net and a water glass (an upside down wooden bucket with a glass bottom) were used to see in the water and locate the catch. Today, most crawfishing for sport or private consumption is done with a mask, snorkel and fins, plus a Hawaiian Sling, the only spear fishing apparatus allowed in the Bahamas. Commercial crawfishing continues to employ small boats, but they are supported by a "mother ship" that serves both as a storage facility for the catch and a home-away-from-home for fishermen on a trip that may last months. In an interview, Captain Andre Sands, a fishing boat owner and Captain for a quarter-century, described the emergence of small "lobster condominiums," containers about the size of a standard pallet and open at the ends. Lobsters crawl Into the "condos" and set up housekeeping. The condos are initially good for the lobster population as juvenile lobsters are protected from predators. Lobsters eventually come to regret their choice of housing as the "condominiums" are GPS tagged and fishermen donning air hoses and a hook return later to scoop up adult lobsters.

Although still plentiful, spiny lobsters have decreased in number and fishermen indicate they now range farther to fill their boats. The lobster is a precious cultural commodity to the Bahamian people, is the country's largest export, and the industry employs

The Long poles, net and water glass have been replaced by a mask, swim fins and a Hawaiian Sling. *(Drawing from a book "Bahamian Sailing Craft," by W.R. Johnston Jr. used with permission. This delightful book depicting historical wooden craft is available at White Sound Press.)*

thousands of people. A 2009 government assessment identified concerns about the sustainability of the fishery. Specifically: unregulated fishing, poor regulation enforcement and data collection, and monitoring were cited for the population decline. It is anticipated that improved enforcement training and capabilities, new reporting requirements, and the establishment of a new harvest control rule will stop the decline.

Hopefully, the fishery improvements will all work, and this important economic and cultural icon will be preserved for fishermen and school kids alike. We hope "Ole Spiny" hangs around another 110 million years!!

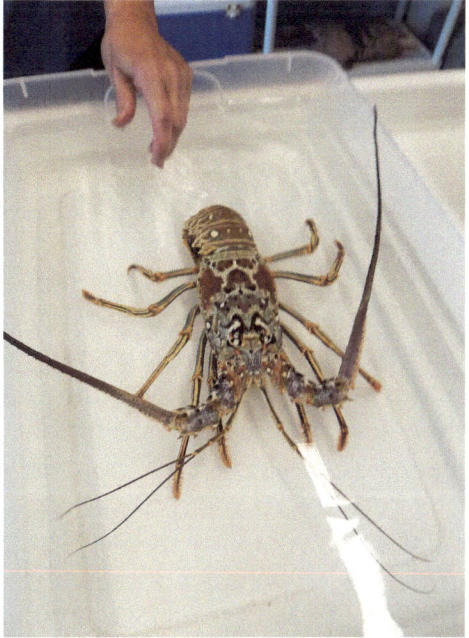

Spiny lobster fishing boat "Bahama Seas" Captain Randy Sawyer has fished Bahamian waters for over fifty years. He was upbeat about his future and supports conservation measures designed to protect the long term lobster population and the fishing industry. Unfortunately, "Bahama Seas" was badly damaged during Hurricane Dorian. Though not destroyed, the boat's future status is unknown.

The Spiny lobster is a fascinating marine animal. For readers who haven't met the "beast," here he is. He's a feisty little devil and a favorite with school kids! (Photo courtesy of the Children's Traveling Zoo, University of Florida's Whitney Laboratory for Marine Bioscience, Marineland, Florida.)

Chapter 7: MailBoat II
Voyage of Legacy

For MailBoat II our crew grew to seven, as the old mailboat hands took on some youngsters. Mike, our baby, was only seventy! Having ridden mailboats before, we were a bit more knowledgable this time and had at least our first trip organized. We had exchanged emails with the Dean Shipping Company, owner of several boats including the mail vessel *Legacy,* and we were on their schedule. Described further in Chapter 11, the Deans are an iconic mailboat family, having been in the business for 70 years. Dean spokeswoman, Kendra Whylly, a sweet lady to be sure, arranged our visit and our voyage was scheduled for departure on February 12, 2018 to Marsh Harbour in the Abaco Islands. *Legacy* is a modern mailboat, built for the trade. Her name commemorates the long Dean mailboat history started by Captain Ernest Dean, who began in the mailboat trade in 1951. The family is still at it as we met Ernest Dean, a son, and Myron Ernest Dean, a grandson who carry on the family tradition. Other family members are also involved in the mailboat business and I would meet them later. The patriarch lived to see his "legacy" grow before he passed in 2010 at age 95. The legacy continues.

Arriving from several states, we seven congregated in Nassau. After arrival, Captain Ernest Dean Jr, met us at the boat for a preliminary tour. Legacy Captain Ricky Barnett showed us around and we picked out our bunk beds for the coming trip. We arrived early on the morning of departure. We looked forward to experiencing once again the "havoc" that is Potters Cay and watch the Legacy load. Tuesday is the busiest mailboat departure day and Potters was a virtual choreography of cargo handling activity with items of every description arriving in every conceivable type of vehicle. The "load" is a big part of the mailboat experience, and we watched it all afternoon.

M/V Legacy loads for departure at Potters Cay. Watching the load is part of the fun!!!

We were invited onboard an hour before our 6 pm departure. Our carry-on suitcases were palletized for the trip and we carried the few essentials we would need for the overnight trip in backpacks. Captain Ricky showed us to our rooms, and we were underway in

Nassau Harbour as the Sun touched the horizon. We would see Ole Sol again in the very early morning as we approached Man-Of-War Cut, the deep ocean passage between Man-O-War and Great Guana Cays into the Sea of Abaco, where several popular Bahama Islands are located in close proximity. We had enjoyed the trip, getting to know both the crew and the other passengers as we all had dinner together, then spent a comfortable night. It would prove to be our favorite trip as the Dean family and the *Legacy* crew took great care of us!

Captain Ricky Barnett, Fred on the bridge of Legacy, our room for the night!!

Sunrise aboard Legacy in Man-O-War Cut!

Great Abaco Island and Nearby Cays:

In mailboat travel, most routes are 7-18 hours and are best begun at dusk for an early morning arrival at the destination. This is especially important if you don't have anywhere to stay when you get there. Later in the trip we would experience how important that timing would be. *Legacy* left Potters Cay on time, and after a pleasant night, we arrived in Marsh Harbour, Great Abaco Island, in the early morning as scheduled. We soon caught the water taxi to nearby Elbow Cay and its main settlement of Hope Town.

We were met at the town dock by the Hope Town Hideaways rental agency who transported the seven of us to our rented beach house to the south of town. We found a beautiful four-bedroom home and two golf carts waiting for us as promised and we'd spend an idyllic week there.

Our beach house on Elbow Cay and
our "rides" in the drive.

83

Navigating around the one bad weather day in the entire trip, we explored old haunts for me and new delights for most of the crew. Late one morning, we drove to Hope Town Harbour Lodge dock and were picked up by the Hope Town Inn and Marina sea shuttle for lunch and a hike to the Elbow Reef Lighthouse. Hope Town is separated by the harbor and a long creek that prevent vehicular traffic from one side to the other. Boats are the only way to travel across the harbor and for the price of lunch, the shuttle is happy to come and get you and take you back later.

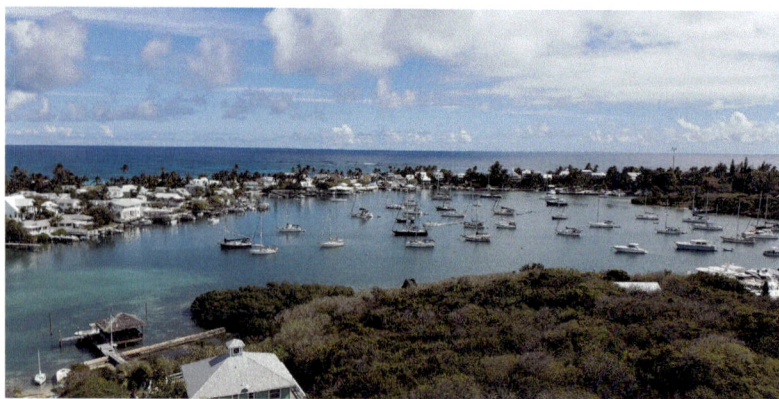

Hope Town Harbour. You need a boat to get across it!

Bahamian Interlude - the Elbow Reef Lighthouse

In one of the planet's great backdrops, the Elbow Reef Lighthouse towers over the harbor and Hope Town. The most recognizable landmark in Abaco, the iconic lighthouse is one of the last manual lighthouses in the world. The lamp burns pressurized kerosene oil with a wick and mantle. The Fresnel lenses concentrate the mantle's light into a beam directed straight towards the horizon. The lighthouse keeper on duty must wind up the weights every 2 hours in order for the light on the red and white candy-striped lighthouse to rotate and be seen from 17 miles away. Steve Dodge writes in "Abaco, The History of an Out Island and Its Cays," the lighthouse was built by the British Imperial Lighthouse Service in 1863." Today the lighthouse is Hope Town's tourist business centerpiece, but it wasn't always that popular. In the 1860s, Elbow Cay residents did their best to prevent its construction. In the mid-nineteenth century, half of the able-bodied men in the Bahamas

Dave Blake Photography

were "wreckers," seamen who salvaged merchant ships that piled up on Elbow Reef. Dodge writes that "Wrecking played an important role in the economy, providing an inexpensive source of imported items, and produced goods for export to the United States and England." Simply stated, lighthouses were bad for business!

The Lighthouse Preservation Society successfully prevented the light from being automated in 1996.

Abaconians are proud of their lighthouse and its history. The government may try to automate it again, but they'd better bring an army!

MailBoat II Crew on top of Elbow Reef Lighthouse

After the lighthouse tour, we encountered several Abaco Dinghies near the lighthouse dock. Roads weren't common in Abaco until the 1990s. Sailing dinghies were the primary mode of transport between the small communities and they still are in many places in the Bahamas. Two of the dinghies were built by the famous Hope Town craftsman, Winer Malone. Also on display at the lighthouse is Winer's last, built in 2010. I tried to see Winer on a previous visit, but he was old and sick and soon passed away. I regret the loss of the opportunity. His dinghies are easy to spot, so pretty.

Bahamian Interlude - Abaco Dinghies

Throughout history and continuing today, Bahamians have depended on boats. Even on large

86

islands with several communities, transportation between populated areas was by boat. The telegraph and later telephones improved communication, but they didn't come to most of the Bahama Islands until fairly recently. There were some footpaths, but no roads. Even the well-established Great Abaco Island didn't have a main road connecting communities along its long, narrow length until the early 1990s when Great and Little Abaco Islands were finally joined by a paved road from the northwest tip of Little Abaco to the southern area of Great Abaco. Besides basic transportation, boats also figured prominently in people's livelihoods and still do. Fishing smacks, spiny lobster or crawfishing boats, sponge schooners, sailing freight boats, and small sail-powered dinghies all contributed to the movement of people, material, information and news. There was even a doctor's office in a sloop! Even today, in some Bahamian locales, nothing much has changed in over two hundred years. Boats remain important in daily life throughout the islands. By necessity, wooden boat-building became a centerpiece of Bahamian society. Several boat building centers in the Abaco Islands, Harbour Island in Eleuthera and in Nassau were prominent.

Though wooden sailing vessels have largely given way to fiberglass and steel, one wooden boat has persisted and is now a still operating collector's item - the Abaco Dinghy. People seeing them for the first time are immediately taken by them. With stylish lines, full keels and wineglass transoms, Abaco dinghies are more like "cute little ships" or scaled-down versions of the bigger Abaco fishing smacks than actual dinghies for harbor transport or towing behind yachts.

It is not known for certain when the Abaco dinghy was first built and emerged as a small fishing and work boat and water taxi, but the type has been around since the 1800s. Built of native hardwoods, most of their breed are 12 or 14 feet long overall with a five-foot beam and a two-foot draft, perfect for the shallows prevalent on the Bahama Banks. The dinghies have a catboat rig on an unstayed mast and a single, large, three-sided sail, nearly the length of the boat. In recent times, Abaco boatbuilders like Maurice Albury on Man-O-War Cay and Winer Malone on Elbow Cay built hundreds of the dinghies for fishing and transportation. Later, yachtsmen started showing up to sail in the Sea of Abaco - sheltered waters lying between the outer Abaco Cays and a barrier reef to the east and Great Abaco Island to the west. The yachtsmen provided a profitable market for the stylish little vessels to be used as daysailers and racers. Dinghy designs are not standard. Each builder has his own variation, as some builders favor sailing performance while others cargo capacity. The Abaco dinghy also became a model for a prominent cousin, Captain Nathaniel Herreshoff's famous 12-foot daysailer, built in the early twentieth century in his boat works in Bristol, Rhode Island.

The appearance of mass-produced and inexpensive fiberglass runabouts greatly diminished demand for the meticulously hand-crafted Abaco dinghy made of wood. It can be argued that the advent of the outboard motor had a greater technological impact on the Bahamas than did the wheel! In any event, demand for the hand-crafted beauties fell sharply. Luckily, there are pockets of resistance to progress. The Hope Town Sailing Club, local lovers of traditional Bahamian small craft, have been reviving the fleet of Abaco dinghies. In the United States, boatbuilding programs are teaching a new generation of boatwrights how to build and sail the Abaco dinghy.

Abaco Dinghy "Dandy," built by Wincr Malone of Hope Town in 1980. Photo courtesy of Jay Fleming.
(www.jayflemingphotography.com)

Today, classic-boat aficionados go to great lengths to get an Abaco dinghy. You can still have a new one built in the traditional way, or you can possibly find an old one to refurbish as many thousands were built. The price tag is a bit north of $20K for either option! Having already established a secure place in Bahamian and nautical history, we can only hope that the Abaco Dinghy will last forever, or at least another two hundred years.

The Sea of Abaco:

The next day we took a "Froggies" snorkeling trip. Froggies is Hope Town's dive operator, and I have a collection of his tee shirts in my closet. This trip was to Sandy Reef to the south of Hope Town. We would snorkel in the protected Sea of Abaco and later continue on to Little Harbour for lunch. It's one of my favorite trips and I knew that even the non-snorkelers would love the ride.

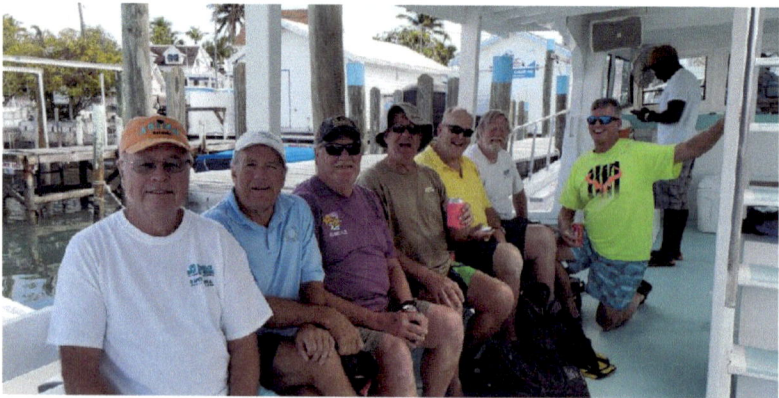

The "MailBoat II Crew" aboard Froggies dive boat. Left to right: Fred, Mike, Dave, Jim, Phil, Jack and Don.

Sandy Reef is shallow and scuba divers have no

advantage over snorkelers as in most places the reef is a few feet below the surface. We spent an hour enjoying the colorful coral reef and tropical fish. "Fred," the reef shark who usually occupies the spot, was absent that day, but a couple of turtles

"Froggies" Dive at Sandy Reef. The colorful reef is in shallow water and easy for snorkelers to explore.

happened by. Our pal Phil did get caught in the current and with his recently installed knee was unable to work his fins hard enough to make any headway. The then anchored dive boat was spared a rescue as he was towed back by a teenager in a small motorboat!

Little Harbour is among the most remote Bahamian communities. I've been here many times, twice on my Catalina 30 *Rhombus.* Sailing from Spanish Wells in Eleuthera to the Abaco Islands, Little Harbour is the closest harbor of safety after a long ocean voyage. It's a dicey entry, but one with few options. It's one of my favorite stretches in the Sea of Abaco, but this time I didn't have to worry about the rocks, coral heads, and other bad things to run into. The Captain from Froggies Tours was driving the dive boat and I just sat back and watched it all happen. Not connected by a road until the mid-1990s, Little Harbour was settled in the 1950s by an "escapee college art professor" who

91

came here to raise his family in peace and pursue his art. Today, Little Harbour is still pretty sleepy and is best known for "Pete's Pub and Art Gallery," as the professor's son Pete carries on his father's artwork in metal sculpture while operating an isolated, but lively bar and grill.

Dave Blake Photography

Bahamian Interlude - Artist on His Island

Canadian artist Randolph Johnston quit his job as a college professor in the early 1950s and traveled to the Bahamas with his family. He purchased a former lobster fishing schooner, loaded his family aboard and set out searching for the perfect spot to live life and pursue his art - sculpture in metal. Randolph had become disillusioned with the world as he saw it, had no real interest in teaching, and just wanted to create art and raise his young family apart from what he termed "the megamachine" of the Western world. We can glean some insight into his thoughts from his published diary, "An Artist on His Island - A Study in Self-Reliance:"

"The prospects for the human species, for the continuation of civilization, appear to me to be very tenuous."

"Day by day, social disintegration seems to loom nearer. Modern man yearns for Eden. Deep in his heart is the nostalgia for the golden age when man was free to live his own life in a beautiful garden."

"Here in pure surroundings, yet facing the responsibilities of coping with nature and life, perhaps our boys will become good men."

This was in the 1950s! One can only wonder how Randolph would feel today!

Randolph, his wife Margot, an artist in ceramics, and young sons Bill, Denny and Pete set sail in their schooner "Langosta" to find the perfect place to build their lives. The family considered and debated the merits of many locales: other parts of the Caribbean, the West Indies, Cuba, Haiti, and the South Sea Pacific Islands. They finally decided on the Bahamas, exactly where they were. After a search and following leads received from other travelers, they eventually landed in Little Harbour on the southeastern coast of Great Abaco Island and selected it for their future island paradise. The area had many beneficial physical attributes and, except for a lighthouse keeper and his family, nobody else was there. In those days in the Bahamas, you could homestead unoccupied Crown land, build a future and stay. Randolph and his family stayed! It took several years to build their future, living for a time aboard Langosta, then later in a nearby cave and in makeshift beach structures. After several years of homesteading struggles and using the income from a small charter business, the family finally established a permanent presence. A studio and foundry were also built to support their art. By any measure, Little Harbour is a most unlikely place for a foundry!

Talent took over and the family went on to achieve international fame as artists, using the 5000-year-old "lost wax" method in the casting of their bronze sculptures. Their art is sold in prestigious art galleries around the world. Randolph's work reflected a philosophical underpinning and he believed that art and morality were linked:

"I am on the side of the individual against oppression in his fight for intellectual, spiritual and moral freedom."

One of Randolph's most notable pieces, "St. Peter: Fisher of Men," rests in the Vatican Museum in Rome. Possibly his most famous work cast in bronze to commemorate the sacrifices of the "Afro-Bahamian Woman," can be seen in Nassau's cruise ship port near Rawson Square. Randolph was pleased with the life he had created. The family's experience might be summed up by Randolph's own words:

"On this particular desert island, life seems to nurture dreams as well as fulfill them."

Although Randolph preferred making art to teaching art, he did teach his sons. He has passed on since giving me a tour of his island home during my first trip to Little Harbour in the late 1980s, but son Pete carries on the family art, while also watching over the

"Afro-Bahamian Woman," by Randolph Johnston

other family enterprise, Pete's Pub and Gallery! A third
generation of Johnstons are in work at Little Harbour.

Pete's son Gregory and his wife Heather operate the pub, boat services and vacation rentals, giving Pete the time to concentrate on his art. Randolph would be pleased!

You can buy Randolph and Pete's work in the family gallery. Go to Little Harbour and see wonderful bronze sculptures on a beautiful and still isolated ocean beach. Then go have a cold one!

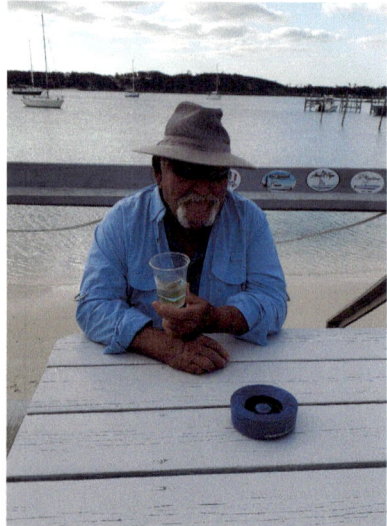

**Pete Johnston,
Little Harbour**

"Aquarius," by Pete Johnston, watches over the ocean beach at Little Harbour."

During a 2020 interview, Pete was asked: "What do you remember most as a six-year-old adventurer?"

"Mosquitoes!"

When our afternoon at Pete's was over, we enjoyed a nice boat ride back to Hope Town. I was again relaxed as we dodged the many rocks. It was a great "Froggies" day! The next day, we again took the Froggies boat, this time to Great Guana Cay. Great Guana is located twelve miles to the north of Hope Town and also in the "Sea of Abaco." The event was Pig Roast Sunday at "Nippers," the famous watering hole perched on a bluff overlooking a beautiful Atlantic Ocean beach.

Great Guana Cay has two personalities. The island is really sleepy, except for the famous Nippers bar and a few other places. Although several high-profile resorts and vacation homes have been added in the past several years, you will still find that out-island charm. If a raucous bar is your style, Nippers is easy walking distance or you can call for the "Nippers-mobile" on VHF radio. If it's quiet you seek, sit on a bench under the famous harbor-side Fig Tree, Great Guana's meeting place. Enjoy a cold drink from the convenience store next door and chat with passers-by. After a spell under the Fig Tree, we strolled along the harbor-front to the Nippers sign and walked up the hill to the Atlantic side of the island. Nippers is active rain or shine, especially on Pig Roast Sunday. A huge party was in full swing when we arrived with barbecued pork to boot. Nippers on any Sunday afternoon is most likely the world's premier people-watching place! The afternoon sped by.

We would spend one more nice day on Elbow Cay, visiting White Sound a few miles south of Hope Town! White Sound is a small and picturesque community with beautiful beaches and nice homes tucked in the sandy hills with flags on poles flapping in the sea breeze. As a Jacksonville Jaguar fan, one flag in particular got my attention! Go Jags!

Dave Blake Photography

Nippers Beach Bar and Grill - People-watching Paradise!!

A Jacksonville Jaguars flag gets a prominent display!

Chapter 8: Island Link
Great and Little Exuma Islands

After a great stay in Abaco, we returned to Mailboat Heaven at Potter's Cay and headed south on our second mailboat for this trip. This time aboard *M/V Island Link* bound for Georgetown and another early morning arrival, so we thought! Island Link is a little smaller than Legacy, but also carries drive-on-drive-off cargo and the passenger facilities are similar. The scenario was the same, leave in the evening and complete the 14 hour trip by the early morning. Perfect! Unfortunately, it didn't go that way.

Dave Blake Photography

We watched the hours-long loading from a perch above it all. As always with mailboats, loading can only be described as fascinating! The photos describe the scene. We boarded on schedule, getting to the boat at the first moment travelers were allowed on board. There are a few rooms with bunk beds, but they are assigned by first-come-first-served. For our scheduled 14 hour trip direct to Georgetown with a 6 pm departure, we

Dave Blake Photography

Dave Blake Photography

Watching the load! Jim is in charge!!

wanted a room! First on board, we got the three rooms we needed, each with two beds instead of the usual six. Rooms were comfortable and my top bunk even had an opening port window! Island Link left an hour late, but, conditions were good and we looked forward to our early morning arrival. Occasionally, I peered out of my opening port at a gorgeous full Moon that was up all night and well into the next morning.

I finally signed off after reading a few chapters of *"Out-Island Doctor,"* a wonderful story about one doctor's adventures in rural Bahamian settlements.

Bahamian Interlude - "Evans Cottman, Out Island Doctor"

Even today, eighty percent of all Bahamians live in five communities and seventy percent of those live in

Nassau. As the population grew after World War II, more Bahamians migrated to the Bahamas Out-Islands (out of Nassau), now called the "Family Islands." Though more people found themselves living in places like Cabbage Hill, True Blue and Abraham's Bay, population support services in those communities were slow to emerge. None were slower to arrive than medical care.

For nearly all Bahamian history, any semblance of professional medical care was available only in Nassau. As late as 1913, only three qualified doctors were practicing in the Out-Islands and nearly ninety percent of that population was not served by any doctor. In the early 1900s, the Bahamian government tried to fill the medical gap by authorizing "Unqualified Licensed Practitioners," persons with a scientific educational background who were authorized to provide general medical care, short of surgery. Near the end of his own long career, "Dr." Robert Stratton met a high school biology teacher from the United States named Evans Cottman, who was spending summers preparing for an early retirement in the Bahamas. With a masters degree in biochemistry, Cottman had the requisite scientific background. Stratton, himself an "Unqualified Licensed Practitioner," was originally from Jamestown, New York and had come to Abaco as a missionary. At Stratton's urging, Cottman didn't retire, instead becoming the "Out-Island Doctor."

Cottman had previously bought a piece of land called Gun Bluff on Crooked Island in the southern Bahamas where he was building a home. Needing water transportation, Cottman traveled to the Abaco Islands to have an Abaco Dinghy built for him. It was there he met Stratton. He also met Viola, the daughter of the homeowner who rented him a room and she would become his wife less than a year later. Cottman retired from his mid-western high school teaching job in 1945 and took his $28.63 monthly school pension and his new bride to Crooked Island. En route, he stopped in Nassau and applied for an "Unqualified Practitioners License," and then quickly forgot about it.

Busy building a new home on a remote island, Cottman's license finally arrived, by mailboat to be sure. Prior to his official "doctor" designation, buying the supplies, medical books and instruments from a deceased physician was the extent of his medical preparation. Nevertheless, when word got out that a "doctor" lived at Gun Bluff, Cottman had an instant practice. A few initial treatment successes made him locally famous. In his autobiography, "Out-Island Doctor," Cottman describes his route to becoming a doctor as the "reverse" of the normal process.

"Most doctors start out by studying medicine. Then they become interns and gradually acquire a practice. After years, they may become famous. My medical career was reversed. I was famous overnight, I immediately had more practice than I could handle, I never went to medical school, I studied medical books between patients, and much later I finally became an intern!"

Cottman's practice spread to nearby islands. He rode mailboats whenever possible and also used dinghy transportation, even over long open ocean stretches. He walked when water travel wasn't possible. His friend's horse "Shadow" was fitted with saddlebags that carried drugs, instruments and medical books. He would often be gone for weeks and regardless of where he went, the extraordinarily effective Bahamian grapevine shouted, "The doctor done reach," spreading notice of his presence far and wide. He treated indigestion, extracted teeth, set broken bones, soothed burns, stopped bleeding, bandaged wounds and "sounded" every patient. All Bahamian patients insisted on being checked with a stethoscope to ensure that "the blood was running right." That the treatment was for an ingrown toenail was inconsequential to the sounding requirement! He also intervened with authorities to arrange transportation to Nassau for patients requiring surgery or were too sick for him to deal with properly. After practicing for a couple of years, Cottman recognized his deficiencies and sought to serve an unofficial "internship" at the hospital in Nassau. Though ignored as an interloper by the larger Nassau medical community, Cottman was taken under the wing of a noted surgeon and he finally received the practical instruction he never had.

Though Cottman loved Gun Bluff and Crooked Island, Viola longed for a return to her family and friends on her native Great Abaco Island and they moved to the region's capital at Marsh Harbour. Though he quickly accumulated a large practice on Great Abaco and surrounding cays, Cottman soon expressed the same sentiment that initially motivated his move to Crooked Island:

"My hunger was for the small, unfrequented, out-of-the-way places."

Cottman's solution to expanding the reach of his practice and experiencing the adventure that went along with it was a thirty-one foot ketch he had built and named the Green Cross. Taught to sail by Viola's Uncle Willie, the boat would become his floating office and for the next three decades he visited the small and isolated communities scattered over hundreds of miles of Bahama Islands. He practiced medicine, but also

103

weathered hurricanes, groundings and experienced the sailing delights and the calamities that those who venture far from shore in small boats know well. Not only is Out-Island Doctor an exciting tale of Cottman's life, it's a gripping account of life in the Out-Islands mid-way through the last century, and to some extent, continuing today.

"Doctor" Evans Cottman sailed and treated patients in his ketch "Green Cross" until his death in 1976. (Drawing courtesy of Steve Dodge)

I have a special attachment to Evans Cottman. I too have spent decades sailing the Bahamas and also prefer the "little places." While reading his words, I had the added thrill of recognizing his travel descriptions, having sailed to many of those places myself over the past thirty years.

Georgetown:

I was up at sunrise to witness the entry into Georgetown. The boat would head further south to Long

Island after dropping us off. A problem; minutes before Ole Sol's daily initial appearance and our scheduled arrival time, we were still far at sea and not heading toward the Exuma chain that lined our port side and contained our destination city. Translation, we were going somewhere else! Ahh, mailboat travel strikes again! Sea conditions dictated that we go to Long Island first, some 60 miles south of Georgetown. Not only would that add 120 miles to our trip, there would be two more unload/reload evolutions as there were two stops in Long Island! We'd experience a second sunset, and maybe a second sunrise before arrival at our destination.

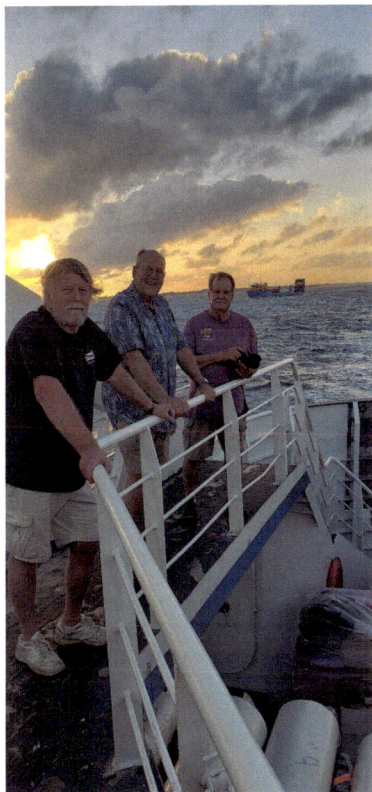

As the Sun sets, Island Link heads south with the MailBoat II Crew paying close attention. A second mailboat trails behind.

Fearful that we would be a day late reaching our reserved hotel, several passengers with local cell phones tried to verify our reservation with no success. The Tourist Bureau in Long Island also tried to help as we approached that Island. Incredibly, the office remembered they had helped us during MailBoat I, two years prior! Is that a testimony to their great memory or

105

something else? Although it looked grim at the time, this too would turn into a typically delightful Bahamian experience.

Our immediate concern was not lodging, but food. Expecting an after-dinner departure with a before-breakfast arrival, I departed Nassau with a snack of two bananas and two oranges purchased at a fruit stand in Potters Cay. Eventually, I would share those as hungry passengers shared what they had! Unlike other mailboats in our experience, *Island Link* did not feed passengers and could have cared less, very un-Bahamian like. They didn't even tell us they were skipping Georgetown until it became obvious. Enter our first Bahamian rescue! Pedrick Dickson, a Bahamas Defense Force Seaman, came aboard to conduct a routine safety inspection at the first stop in Long Island. Overhearing a discussion of our hunger discomfort, he rushed us in his car to find food, getting us back to the ship before departure. Finding a little neighborhood cafe, we took double cheeseburgers back to eleven passengers, all starving!

After our second sunset, we arrived in a port in the boonies some miles from Georgetown at 3 am. Nothing much was around. Bahamian Patrick Davis, a fellow traveler who lived nearby, recognized our plight and took us home! "Honey, I'm bringing home six big guys I just met to spend the night!" Try that one at home! By the time we arrived, the living room was made into a dorm with an inflatable bed surrounded by a big couch and three overstuffed chairs. I took a chair, knowing it wouldn't matter where I slept, as tired as I was! In the morning, Patrick's girlfriend Amanda Robinson found us a ride into town to search for our villas. Once we finally found the "Bay Villas," we discovered why none of our helpers could contact them; nobody was there!

The Mailboat "crew" asleep in Patrick's living room. Patrick and Amanda were great hosts!!

Homeless once again during peak tourist season, the local Tourist Bureau came to our rescue, finding us a delightful oceanfront place. We had a great time with the kids though we were "attacked" by a group of pirates from an off-shore fleet during our stay. No hostages were taken, and they made a clean get-away!

Pint-sized pirates make a hasty retreat after attacking our hotel and occupying the pool!

We had a great time in Georgetown, exploring the lengths of Great and Little Exuma Islands from Barraterre in the far north of Great Exuma to Williams Town on the southern end of Little Exuma. From Barraterre you can catch the tour boats to some of the small Exuma Cays. Little Exuma is connected to the larger island by a one-lane bridge. Traveling the smaller island to its end, we passed the Great Salt Ponds, the site of a salt harvesting area that was a commercial hit during times when salt was used as a food preservative. We spent our last Georgetown day on popular Stocking Island, where the "cruising fleet" mixes with day trippers. In a pure-party atmosphere, we enjoyed a terrific last Exuma day. Later that day we would return to Nassau and Potters Cay for most of us to catch the last MailBoat, *Fiesta Mail*.

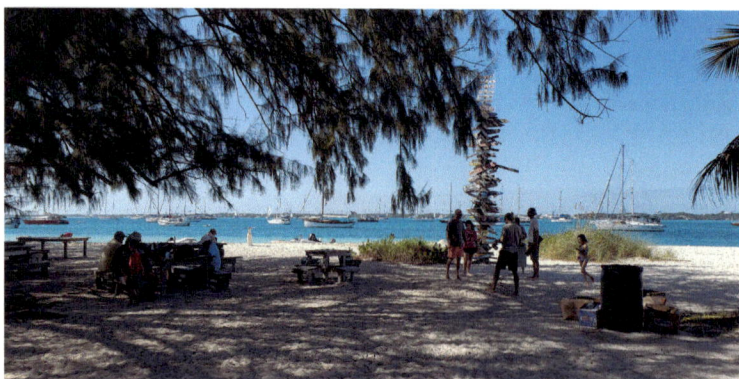

Stocking Island, a small, sandy island across from busy Georgetown, collects day trippers and the yachting crowd anchored nearby. The island's only restaurant and bar is appropriately named "Chat 'N' Chill!"

Bahamian Interlude - "The Great Salina"

While exploring Great and Little Exuma Islands, we happened upon a tall Tuscan style pillar on the edge of a beautiful Little Exuma shoreline. The pillar marked a little bay that guided 18th and 19th Century sailing ships into an anchorage where they could take aboard one of the era's most valuable commercial products - salt. Due to their very close proximity to the salty ocean, three near-shore ponds on Little Exuma Island had lots of salt, ready for the taking.

Salt is history's food preservative. Before refrigeration became widespread in modern times, salting, or the preservation of food with dry edible salt, was one of the oldest food preservation methods and salt was a hot commercial commodity. Salt was so valuable in hot climates that North Africans once traded measures of gold to Europeans for equal measures of salt. They needed salt but had none and had lots of gold, but had little use for it. Salting is used because most bacteria, fungi and other potentially pathogenic organisms cannot survive in a highly salty environment, or will become temporarily inactivated by it.

The Exumas, like the Bahamas in general, underwent a population boom when "British Loyalists" showed up after the US Revolution. Though they preferred to plant cotton and to continue life as they had known it in the Southern Colonies, they found Exuma inhabitants already engaged in the salt trade. The site had long been known to exist, having been spotted by Loyalist John Darell while hunting whales in the area in 1670. The salt ponds cover more than 200 acres of land where the sea water flows into the shallow near-shore ponds. Sluice gates were eventually added and closed at high tide. The concentrated salt water was moved to shallow areas to continue to dry out and bleach in the hot Bahamian Sun. Evaporation would do its thing and leave behind the salt residue. Rakers working the salt ponds created piles of the stuff, loaded it into baskets

109

for transport the short distance to the bay and the waiting ships. At the peak of the period as many as sixty commercial vessels made up the "salt fleet," trading in the valuable commodity.

One advertisement of the era read:

"For Sale"

From ten to fourteen thousand Bushels of Salt lying contiguous to The Landing on the Great Pond of Little Exuma - a boat to carry 60 Bushels will be furnished and every assistance given for Dispatch.

Nassau January 10, 1789

The bay where the "Salt Fleet" waited and the "Salt Beacon" on the hill that guided their arrival. The largest of the salt ponds is close to the bay just to the right of the column.

The close proximity of the pond on the right and the bay allowed the enterprise to flourish until refrigeration ended the trade.

Sea water still floods the ponds without commercial purpose and only a few local residents and an occasional tourist rake the the ponds for local use or souvenir salt. Unfortunately, the iconic column that for two hundred years guided ships to a "salty" rendezvous is in trouble. The pillar is in need of repair and the cliff on which it stands may soon be undermined by ever-encroaching wave action. After more than 300 years as a landmark, this historic column may end up as a historical pile of rocks.

Chapter 9: Fiesta Mail
"The Final Four," Freeport and Home

Phil and Jim departed for home during our third trip to Nassau, leaving Dave and I and the two youngsters, Mike and Jack, to catch the last mailboat, this time to Freeport, Grand Bahama Island. A fast ferry would take us home to Florida from there. Though MailBoat II was less than forty-eight hours from completion, there was still plenty of time for one more Bahamian adventure. *M/V Fiesta Mail* is the largest of the mailboats and her paint job is a floating advertisement for the industry.

M/V Fiesta Mail passes the Lighthouse departing Nassau Harbour.

This mailboat can carry over 400 passengers and is set up with a large indoor lounge with airline-style seats and big-screen TVs, an outdoor lounge and a snack bar. Unlike the ideal evening departure with a morning arrival, this boat left in the early afternoon and would arrive in Freeport very late the same day. It didn't work out that way, demonstrating once again that mailboat travel demands flexibility!

We boarded when allowed and took up residence in the comfortable lounge for the ten-hour trip.

We knew the arrival in Freeport would be trouble as far as the night's accommodations were concerned. Expecting to arrive before midnight, we had hoped just to stay on board until morning. Our ferryboat ride home was scheduled to depart for Ft. Lauderdale early the next day. But the boat was late into Freeport and expected a quick turnaround. Our plan wasn't possible. Upon arrival at about 3 am, we were homeless once again! Enter Winston and his bus!

For the second week in a row, we arrived in a dark port in an isolated area in the dead of night with no place to go. Winston owned a bus and was contracted to transport passengers from the dock to the passenger terminal, which closed soon after our arrival. After completing his contract duties, he came back, hoping to help find us rooms in a nearby hotel. Failing that Winston, like Patrick the previous week, - can you believe it - took us home! His wife also offered the living

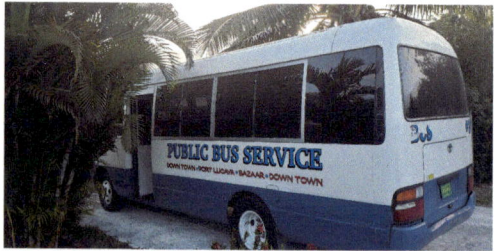

room, but we opted for the bus. Each row with a center seat was a bed and we slept soundly in his driveway!

Winston couldn't find us a hotel, but we spent a comfortable night in his bus!

In the morning, Winston woke us up and took us to Wendy's for breakfast before depositing us at the terminal to catch the *Balearia* Line fast ferry to Ft. Lauderdale. MailBoat II was over and we'd all soon be home. We had a great time and saw a lot of a great country. We suffered some anxious moments, but also experienced the kindness and concern for strangers that you'd wish was prevalent everywhere. We had idyllic days of leisure in our Abaco beach house and the Georgetown resort. We loved touring the islands by land, playing with the kids in the pool, and we enjoyed ourselves immensely. We spent time ashore with

Bahamians and spent days at sea, getting to know boat crews and passengers alike. Mailboat travel is unique and not without its uncertainties. But, if you are a little adventuresome and willing to exchange a bit of travel turmoil for an authentic Bahamian experience, give it a try. You won't get this on a cruise ship!

MB II Summary:
17 days total
6 days at sea
8 islands visited
4 visits to Potters Cay
4 rescues by Bahamians
2 times adopted by Bahamians
Countless personal interactions
Many many stories to tell

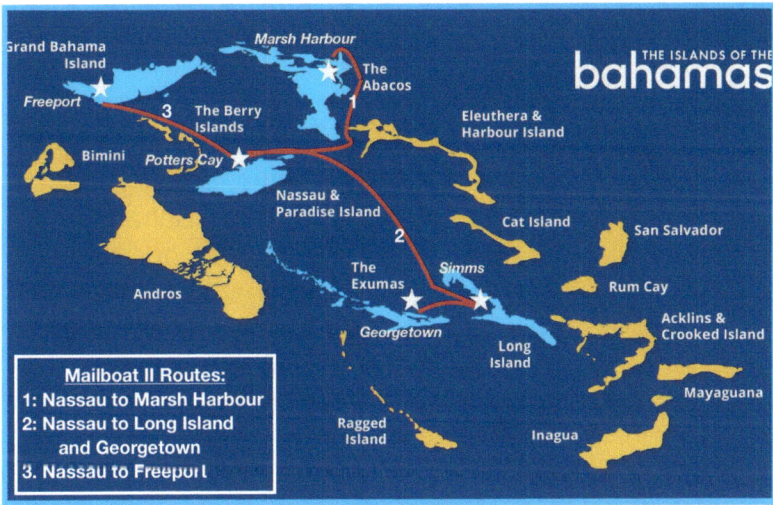

The MailBoat Crews are up to seventeen Bahama Islands visited. Only 683 to go!!

Chapter 10: MailBoat III
Bahamas Daybreak and Return to Eleuthera

MailBoat III started just like the other trips, except a new crew was in place. Perry McDonald is an old sailing friend and Olga Isabelle Copson, is an adventurous lady and a fellow volunteer in a children's marine animal traveling education program. Our plan for this trip was the same as in past trips: make a plan, fly to Nassau over the weekend, visit Potters Cay to talk to mailboat crews, and determine how the plan must change! The plans ALWAYS change. But, in this case the change was slight.

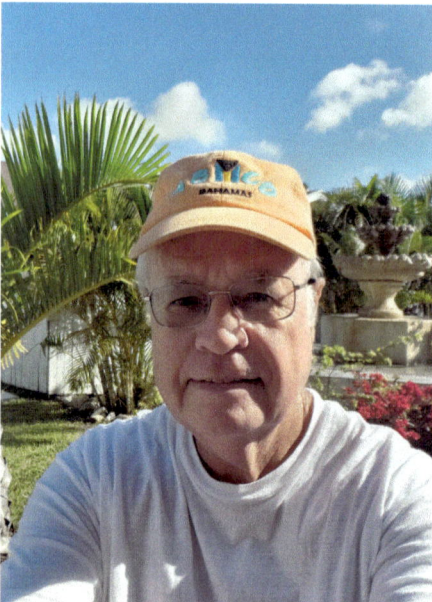

We arrived in Nassau on the same plane, quickly passed through Bahamian Customs and soon collected our rental car. Our destination was the favored mailboat crew quarters at the Colony Club Inn. It's a small mom and pop style inn off the beaten path. With a very interesting multi-ethnic, multi-cultural, international clientele, it's about as far away from area mega-resorts as you can get. But it's so much fun. Arriving about

The Captain at the Colony Club Inn, a very pleasant place!

116

dinner time, we proceeded to the nearby beach strip known as "Fish Fry" for a quick dinner. We returned home in time to catch the last of the Club's 'happy hour' by the pool. In bed by 10, I looked forward to exploring tomorrow and showing the Crew some of Nassau's delights from a frequent visitor's perspective. MailBoat Heaven at Potters Cay, where we hoped to validate our plans for Monday, was our prime destination.

Sunday morning I took Olga to a Greek Orthodox Church loosely affiliated with one she knows in St. Augustine. Perry and I proceeded to Rawson Square where I showed him the metal sculpture "Afro-Bahamian Woman," by Randolph Johnston. After picking Olga up from church, we proceeded to the day's main event, a tour of Potters Cay to check on our plans for the next day. Bring on Plan B! Our intended boat, *Bo Hengy III,* scheduled for an 8 am departure for Spanish Wells, was out of service for a week. Our back up boat was leaving a day later than expected. Options were many: MailBoat *Bahamas Daybreak I* to Spanish Wells and Harbour Island or *Daybreak II* to Governors Harbour, Eleuthera. Both are six or seven hour trips compared to the fast Bo Hengy's two hours. There was also a slower cargo ferry scheduled. Another option, *Captain C* to Ragged Island (almost to Cuba) - a two day trip - via several stops in the Exumas. All demonstrate Mailboat Travel Rule Two once again:

"You can't find out where and when MailBoats are really going without talking to the crew, and even then you can't be sure!"

After arranging for another day at The Colony Club and a nap, we capped off a great day with dinner with the Tate family (David, Crystal, and David junior). The Tates are the Bahamian family my friends and I have

117

raised funds for to help rebuild their Hurricane Dorian ravaged home. We returned to Curley's at Fish Fry and the six of us had a great evening. David Tate told us of his planned new charter fishing business. He lost the one associated with the lodge where he worked, destroyed by the hurricane. He also described and showed videos of his method of catching spiny lobster using a hook and diving gear. Of course I have mixed emotions about this as "spiny" is one of my animals at the Whitney Lab's Traveling Children's Zoo and I love them. But, people need to feed their families.

After a great evening, we looked forward to tomorrow's uncertainty, part of the mailboat travel charm. We spent most of the day enjoying the Potters Cay scene. After watching her load for several hours, we departed as scheduled on *Bahamas Daybreak* for Spanish Wells, Eleuthera. She was our third boat choice but, as it turned out, the best one. Departure was scheduled for 5 pm. This is an unusual trip, because it is short. We would be homeless upon arrival.

Watching a mailboat load is always fun!

Arriving around 10 pm, the boat would stay in Spanish Wells for the night and we asked if we could stay on board until morning when we could look for a place to stay. Sure, $10. Easy decision. We boarded *Bahamas Daybreak* at 2:30 or so. They had a four-bunk room picked out for us. We even had two bathrooms next door, one with an unheard of luxury on a mailboat - a shower! We were underway at five and fed the crew's meal of chicken wings or

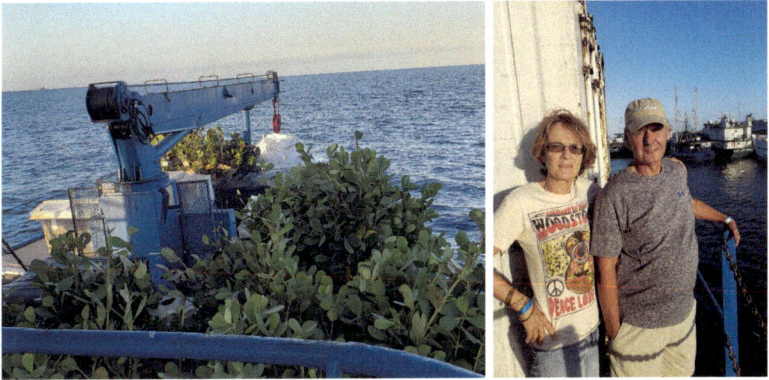

We sped out of Nassau Harbour with several passengers and a full cargo load, including a small forrest!

spaghetti by six. We had a peaceful night, though a little cool without my biker's sleeping bag. So with our home set for the night, we looked forward to tomorrow, certain that it would be different. Early bedtime.

The *Bahamas Daybreak* docked in Spanish Wells around 10 pm, too late to explore town. Remaining on board as planned, the boat started making noise about 5 am, discharging cargo before sunrise - or "daybreak" in this boat's case! So we were off the boat early and with nothing open, we camped out at the water-taxi dock. Our plan was to spend a few days exploring mainland Eleuthera and then return to Spanish Wells for a couple of days before returning to Nassau. Once back in Nassau, we would catch the MailBoat to Sandy Point in the Abaco Islands the next day. At least that was the plan. We were able to reserve a harbor-front motel for our planned return to Spanish Wells. Future accommodations assured, we took the water taxi to Eleuthera and our reserved rental car was driving up to meet us as we arrived. We'd explore Eleuthera for a few days before returning to Spanish Wells and eventually return to Nassau for the second part of our trip.

True to her name, Bahamas Daybreak deposited us at the dock and was leaving Spanish Wells just as Ole Sol started to peek.

Mainland Eleuthera:

We were soon on our way and I looked forward to showing friends some neat things about Eleuthera that I knew well from past sailing trips and MailBoat I. Driving south on Queens Highway (the only highway!), we kept watching for a place to stay for a few nights. We visited the unique Glass Window, called the narrowest place on Earth, where you can look out over both the deep-blue Atlantic and the shallow, aquamarine Exuma Sound. We proceeded south through Hatchet Bay and Alice Town. Both have special places in my sailing memory. We stopped to talk to Emmitt at Farrington's Boaters Haven who owns a restaurant and convenience store in front of my two anchorage spots in 2012 and 2018.

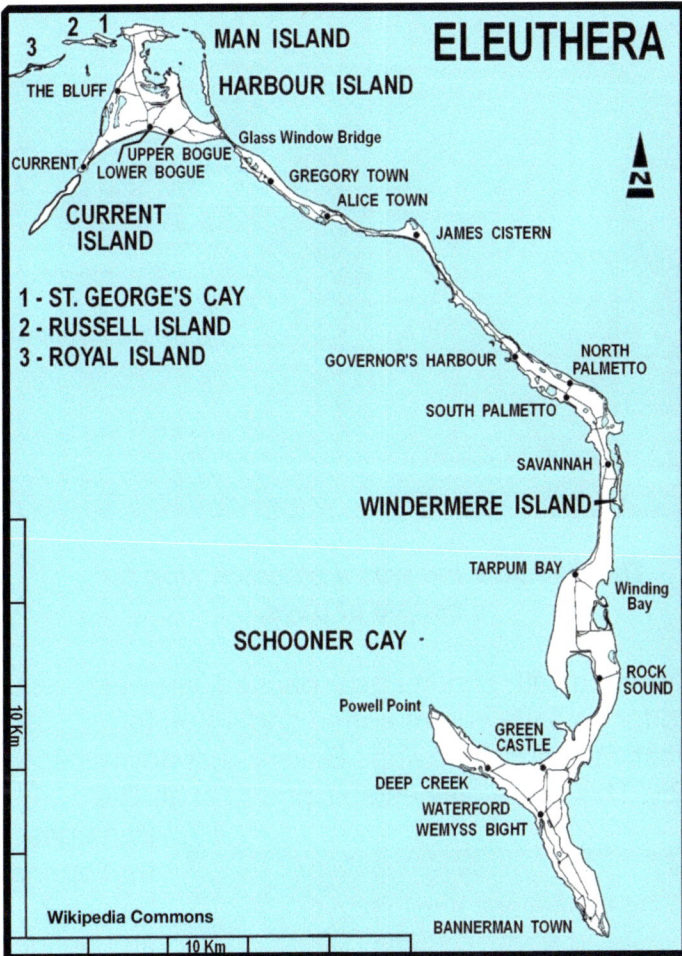

ELEUTHERA

MAN ISLAND
HARBOUR ISLAND
THE BLUFF
Glass Window Bridge
CURRENT
UPPER BOGUE
LOWER BOGUE
GREGORY TOWN
ALICE TOWN
CURRENT ISLAND
JAMES CISTERN

1 - ST. GEORGE'S CAY
2 - RUSSELL ISLAND
3 - ROYAL ISLAND

GOVERNOR'S HARBOUR
NORTH PALMETTO
SOUTH PALMETTO
SAVANNAH
WINDERMERE ISLAND
TARPUM BAY
Winding Bay
SCHOONER CAY
ROCK SOUND
Powell Point
GREEN CASTLE
DEEP CREEK
WATERFORD
WEMYSS BIGHT
Wikipedia Commons
BANNERMAN TOWN
10 Km

Driving or boating along Eleuthera's western shore, you'll find charming places, interesting sights and safe harbors every twenty miles or so.

Still heading south, we encountered Rainbow Bay Inn, a small resort on an Exuma Sound beach. Simple, pretty, inexpensive - just our style. We spent the day there with a little ride to the south. Pizza for dinner and to bed - 7:30 or so. Mailboating can be tiring!

121

The Rainbow Inn was a pleasant stop for a couple of days.

Rested with snorkel gear packed, we went looking for an early cup of coffee and a bun for breakfast. We found Cravings Bakery, just down the highway. This is the only establishment in all The

Bahamas that opens before 9 am! As luck would have it, we arrived just after a "herd" of kids, all students from the Island School.

More about the school later. After collecting our coffee, juice and, in my case chocolate cake, we all had breakfast at picnic tables on the beach.

After a great start to our day, we continued south to Governor's Harbour. The adjacent Cupid's Cay is the site of the first New World republic. Arriving in 1648, the first British settlers in the Bahamas were called "Eleutherian Adventurers." I've been here twice before on *Rhombus*. In 2012, it was on this pretty beach that I first dragged my dinghy ashore to chain it to a tree for safekeeping. In the process, I was admonished by a girl of about seven or eight;

"Mister, nobody is going to steal your little boat!"

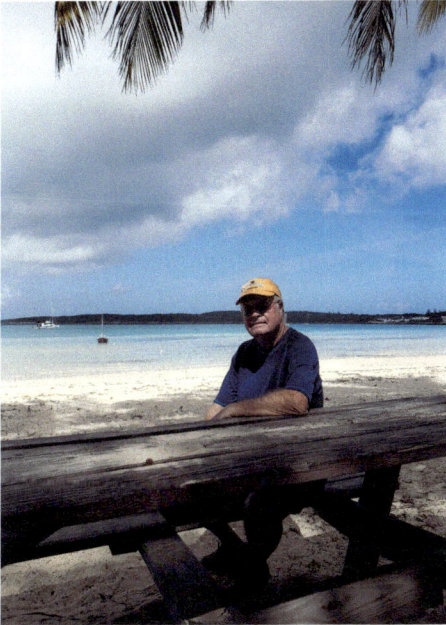

The Captain Resting on Cupid's Cay

Suitably chastised, I dropped the chain and lock in the dinghy and walked off to explore. I saw the young lady later and bought her an ice cream bar. I never locked anything in The Bahamas again.

Still later, we traveled along the coast, stopping at a couple of snorkeling spots. Nice day! Off to dinner at a local spot with Bahamian music tonight.

Bahamian Interlude - The Eleutherian Adventurers

On the heels of New World discoveries by Spanish and Portuguese explorers, Pope Alexander VI issued a "Papal Bull," or decree in 1493 that authorized Spain and Portugal to colonize the Americas. England was left out of all the New World discovery fun. In 1534 King Henry VIII separated from Rome. England was no longer bound by the decree and English colonization started, principally in North America. After Sir Walter Raleigh's ill-fated attempt at Roanoke in 1585, the English finally established their presence with colonies in Virginia, Bermuda and New England between 1607 and 1620.

Religion, as well as British politics, heavily influenced what came next. Britain was embroiled in political turmoil with the short-lived, Oliver Cromwell-led Commonwealth of England. Though Cromwell's Commonwealth lasted only eleven years, it accompanied a religious split between Royalist members of the Church of England and religion reformers; Puritans and others who preached religious tolerance. This conflict followed colonists to Bermuda, which became over populated by the mid-1600s. Enter Captain William Sayle, Bermuda's governor and an advocate of colonization farther south in the largely unpopulated Bahama Archipelago. Sandra Riley in her book "Homeward Bound," states:

"The ordinary colonist had been drawn overseas by the Englishman's desire to better himself."

In those days bettering meant acquiring land. William

Sayle promoted immigration to the Bahama Islands in a pamphlet in 1647. Whether it was religious freedom they sought or just land, Sayle quickly gathered seventy "Adventurers," and set off in two ships in search of a suitable island to begin a new life.

The "Adventurers" sailed south. Sayle had obtained a charter from the king to colonize new lands south of where the Massachusetts Pilgrims had settled. Several weeks after setting sail from Bermuda towards warmer climes, Sayle and his two ships wrecked on the reefs of the northern end of the island, near the area now known as Preachers Cave.

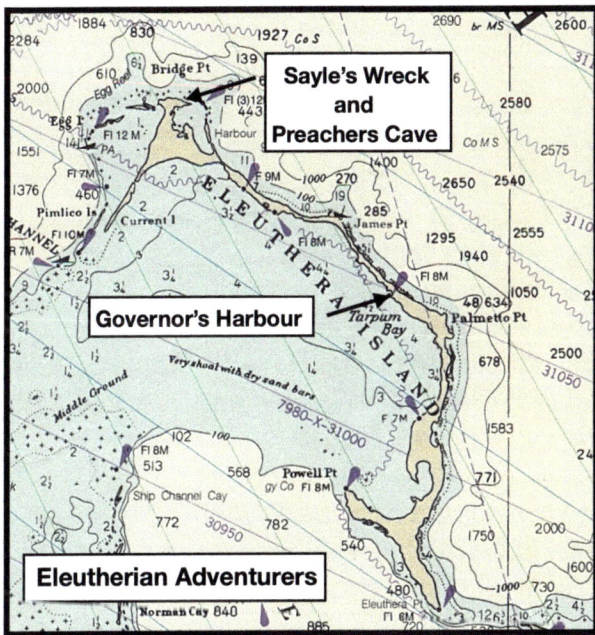

Most managed to swim ashore and find a haven in the large cavern where they reportedly prayed and preached. It was here that the thankful survivors named their island "Eleuthera, the Greek word for freedom."

The newly named "Eleutherian Adventurers," found the island uninhabited. The previous Native population had been killed off by European diseases or

125

carted off by the Spanish to serve as slaves elsewhere in the Caribbean. Though it never lived up to its promise, the "Articles and Orders of Incorporation" of the new colony were, nevertheless, remarkable for their time. The orders guaranteed both freedom of religion and opinion and the establishment of a republic, the first democratic state in the New World. The charter further stipulated that of any Natives found:

"Not to offer them any wrong, violence, or incivility whatsoever, but shall deal with them with all justice and sweetness." It was further stipulated that any Natives found and previously enslaved, should "be then returned to the places from which they were taken."

Eventually, Sayle and his followers made it across the island to a quiet harbour on the coast of what is now Exuma Sound. They set up the first New World republic in 1648 on Cupid's Cay, a small cay located on a large harbor now popular with visiting yachtsmen, including me. Though the timing is unclear to this writer, settlements remained or were established in the north near the original shipwreck in what is now Spanish Wells and Harbour Island. Preachers Cave is now a popular tourist site.

Although the climate was perfect and the island experienced adequate rainfall, the rocky terrain made crop cultivation difficult. Other than seafood, the island lacked natural resources. Some Adventures gave up and returned to Bermuda to beg forgiveness of the King. To rescue his fledgling settlement from starvation, Sayle journeyed west in search of supplies from North American colonies. Driven ashore on an island to the west of Eleuthera, Sayle was fortunate to discover a naturally-protected, deep-water harbor rather than a rocky shore. Called Sayle's Island for many years, the *island is now New Providence and the harbor area's future city is Nassau.*

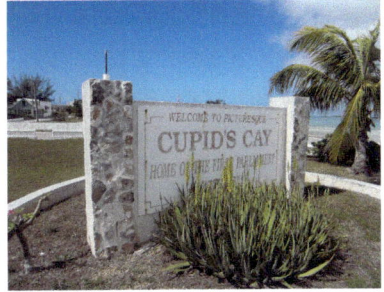

Given the opportunity, area residents will still tell visitors about the "Eleutherian Adventurers."
(Photos by Perry McDonald)

Although the center of Bahamian prominence and commercial life transferred to Nassau long ago, settlements remain surrounding Governor's Harbour. Residents are proud of their heritage and still claim lineage to the original, "Eleutherian Adventurers."

South Eleuthera:

We departed our nice place at the Rainbow Inn, and continued south. We made a brief stop at the Queen's Bath, an interesting oceanside rock formation where visitors swim in rock pools and wait for the big ocean swells to crash the rocky coast, providing an instant bath! We proceeded to Rock Sound where we found a couple of rooms at Sammy's Place, a tiny hotel with four rooms above the kitchen and restaurant. Sammy's Place fit our criteria perfectly, simple and nice. We even spent time in the kitchen with cook Kathleen admiring her recent haul of hot peppers, destined to become Louisiana Hot Sauce. She collects peppers after work on her small farm.

We dropped our stuff at Sammy's and drove out to Cape Eleuthera, stopping first at the Island School to verify our tour appointment for the next day. The Island School is a special school that teaches sustainable living in addition to a standard academic program. We then proceeded on to the Cape Eleuthera Marina. I sailed into this pretty spot in 2012 and 2018. We spent some time at their lovely beach, taking advantage of the marina's WiFi to send a few messages home.

Sammy's Place fit our style and Kathleen showed us her peppers.

For visiting boaters, the Cape Eleuthera Marina is a welcome sight

On the way back to Rock Sound, we stopped off in the nearby town of Green Castle to visit TJ's Bar, a colorful little place next door to the owner's home. Started by TJ's father, the bar is a favored

129

gathering place for residents of the tiny town and is also fun for passing visitors.

The MailBoat III Crew Visits TJ's - a lot of bar in a tiny space.

Back in Rock Sound, we unpacked at Sammy's Place and explored the town. Although not as upscale as The Rainbow Inn, Sammy's is a pleasant spot with inexpensive and clean rooms with a local-feel restaurant and bar below. We relaxed a bit the next morning before taking off for our appointment with the Island School staff and our tour through the school and the adjoining Cape Eleuthera Institute. It would be my third visit to this fascinating place, and I was certain that the MailBoat III Crew would enjoy it. Returning to Rock Sound after the tour, we did some laundry, packed, enjoyed Sammy's bar and the local crowd one last time, and got ready for the next day's change in venue. We would return to Spanish Wells the next day - 80 miles and a ferry ride away. No need to set an alarm for an early departure. Sammy's chickens will take care of that!

Bahamian Interlude - The Island School and The Cape Eleuthera Institute

School Motto: "Don't let school get in the way of your education!"

No trip to Eleuthera's mainland would be complete without visiting "The Island School" and "The Cape Eleuthera Institute." The two organizations work together, share faculty and researchers and are connected by a "rumber" bridge! I discovered The Island School in 2012 during a long trek sailing through the islands. The school teaches and practices "sustainable living" and the Institute figures out how to do it more efficiently. The school is unique to say the least with staff titles like Head Gardener, Bike Shop Head, Fish Farm Supervisor, and Carpenter all included along with the academic titles. I was delighted to make a return visit.

The school is tucked in a mangrove and palmetto forest on the banks of Exuma Sound and is certainly not traditional. Admission is competitive with only about fifty students a term and twenty faculty from all over the world. Two Bahamians receive a scholarship. Founded in 1998, students come for a semester, usually in the 10th or 11th grade. The school's theme is "sustainable living," and they practice what they preach with solar panels, a wind generator, uses for discarded old tires, a small farm with animals, an off-shore fish farm, biodiesel production, and recycled everything. The bridge that connects school and institute campuses is made of "rumber," a composite of recycled car tires and wood from the Casuarina tree, an invasive species that would be nice to eradicate. Their furniture is made of the same wood. It's fitting that the only fish that show up on the school's Casuarina-wood dining tables are farm-grown tilapia and freshly caught lion fish, an invasive critter on the wanted list.

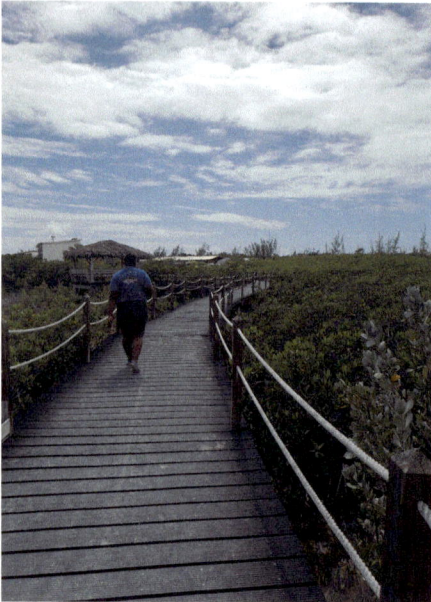

Pass over the Rumber Bridge to go from the School to the Institute.

Other interesting studies and practices of the two organizations that were active during this visit involve hydroponic growing (in water without soil) of vegetables to combat the Bahamas' poor soil, small-scale, back-yard fish farms to provide a needed protein source without further depleting the over-fished surroundings, and the *very strange miracle tree. Juice from the fruit of this tree makes anything you eat after taste good, possibly providing a solution for eating difficulties of patients taking strong medications.*

Students trade a typical high school term for seven days-a-week classes and early-morning reveille with calisthenics. No cell phones or internet are allowed except when used in a class. Students get fifteen minutes a week to call home. All classes have a community field component, and students are outside of class more than in. With an eye toward "growing concern for Planet Earth" in young people, the school operates and students work closely with the Deep Creek Middle School, an independent school for Bahamian students in grades seven through nine. Founded in 2001, the school draws students from eleven Eleutherian communities. With a goal of increasing access to alternative education methods, DCMS was recently recognized by The Bahamas Ministry of Education as a laboratory school for its innovative initiatives and success! One right of passage for Island School students is a half-marathon run or a four-mile ocean swim. Students make their choice early in their term and then train for it throughout their stay. Another requirement for graduation is an overnight, solo kayak-camping trip into the mangroves. They take a handheld VHF radio for real trouble, but it is seldom used. Students also earn PADI's Open Ocean Diving Certification during their stay. I talked to one girl in an English class. "Why are you wearing a bathing suit?" She replied, "I have to work at the fish farm for my next class, and won't have time to change and still catch the boat." It is neat seeing high school kids moving from class to class, with swim fins and a snorkel sticking out of their backpacks! The school's one high school term may well provide a life-changing experience. I think that's the idea. I was present during "graduation week" when parents joined their students on campus. It was clear that, in spite of the program's rigors, nobody wanted it to end. It was great to visit again and see that the school is still going strong. If you will soon have a 10th or 11th grader, check out The Island School at http://www.islandschool.org.

High school scenes are much different at "The Island School," and "The Cape Eleuthera Institute" has many interesting projects.

Spanish Wells:

This was my fourth trip to Spanish Wells - two by sailing through the area and now my second by mailboat. Though I love The Bahamas in general and have a multitude of favorite spots, Spanish Wells is high on the recommended list for first-time Bahamas visitors. Spanish Wells is located in one of the beautiful places on Earth. If wonderful ocean beaches located among multi-colored surrounding waters with dozens of small islands, cays and interconnecting waterways were not enough, the town adds the charm of a working fishing village. We checked in at Harbourside Rentals across from the ferry landing to collect both our motel room key and our golf cart.

Harbourside Motel is in the center of Spanish Wells activity

After depositing our bags at the motel, the Crew took off to explore Spanish Wells' delights for the first time while I revisited old favorites. Spanish Wells hadn't changed in the year since my last visit. The lobster season was in its final weeks, the boats were out, and port activity was at its lowest. The great little boatyard on the harbor was still very active and I quickly located two people I was interested in finding. The pilot A1, who had led me through the reef on two previous sailing trips, was still scooting around town in his golf cart with A1 on the side. His boat with the same notation, however, was gone from its familiar berth in the harbor. Well past 80, A1 had retired. However, Captain Bird, now ninety-three, was still at his job of driving his cart around town looking for people needing a ride! You don't even have to ask. After learning that two old friends were well, I set out to visit old haunts and thankfully found them unchanged also.

A1 isn't piloting boats anymore, but Captain Bird will still pick you up!

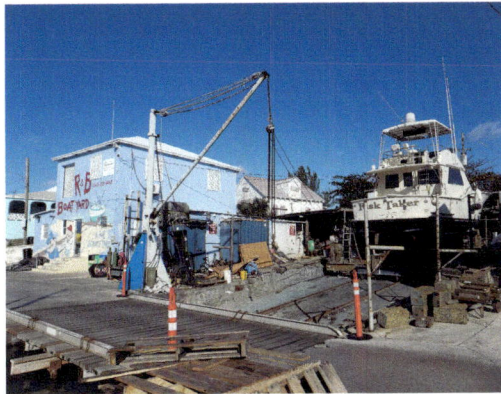

R & B packs a lot of boatyard in a space a little bigger than a normal house lot!

We lounged around another day, spending time at the beach and exploring near-by Russell Island, connected by a small bridge. I also found time to conduct a couple of very informative interviews; one with retired lobster fishing boat Captain

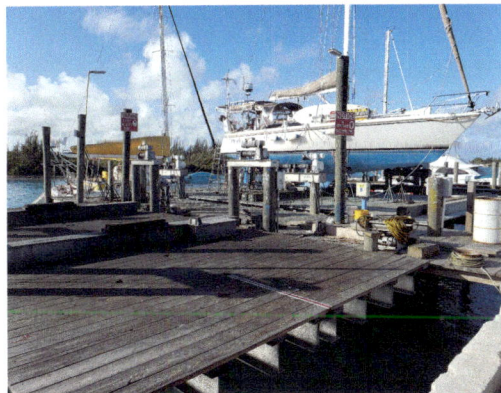

Andre Sands, and one with mailboat owner Billy Pinder. Pinder's former boat, *M/V Eleuthera Express*, was just made into a pirate ship tourist attraction in Nassau. I would find the new version of the boat later.

I snuck in one last trip to the beach and, as late afternoon arrived, we all retired to Budda's Snack Shack for dinner and drinks. We crashed early, mindful of the next day's return to Nassau, by mailboat of course!

Northern Eleuthera beaches are as good as it gets!

Chapter 11: Captain Gurth Dean
Sandy Point and the
Original Ernest Dean Route

We had a quiet morning as our ride for the return to Nassau did not arrive until late afternoon and then almost immediately departed. *The Bo Hengy III* does what all mailboats do, carry mail, people and cargo, with emphasis on people. The cargo rule is simple: you can bring with you anything you can carry up the ramp with a one-person trip. However, I've seen some prodigious loads waddle aboard. The most memorable was a small refrigerator strapped to a gentleman's back! *Bo Hengy III* is also very fast, less than half of a *Bahamas Daybreak* trip back to Nassau.

Bo Hengy III arrived on time and we were headed back to Nassau a few minutes later.

Although we didn't depart Spanish Wells until after 4 pm, we still made the last part of the daily happy hour at the Colony Club Inn in Nassau. Anticipating departure on the second leg of our trip the next day, we ordered pizza and hit the sack early. The next morning, we learned that our boat *M/V Gurth Dean* would be delayed and we wouldn't leave that day after all. Mailboat travel strikes again! Ordinarily we'd just look for another mailboat and go somewhere else, but, I had good reason to make this trip, so we waited. After arranging another day at the Inn, I went back to Potters Cay to verify the schedule, while Perry and Olga went downtown to shop. Arriving at Potters Cay, I headed directly for the Dockmaster's Office and then to the already re-loading *Gurth Dean.* Gurth Dean's Mate Jackie McKenzie verified the new schedule. We would depart the next day at 9 pm.

With a little time on my hands, I walked back to town, searching for the pirate ship *Blackbeard's Revenge*, the former *Eleuthera Express.* I had learned of the transformation from the former owner during our last stop in Spanish Wells. I had also seen and photographed the Express at sea during MailBoat II while traversing the famed Devil's Backbone in Northern Eleuthera. The new incarnation of the ship was easy to find, and I was invited aboard by the operator to take a look after being observed taking photos of the ship.

A "Pirate Ship" has returned to Nassau. The former MailBoat "Eleuthera Express," (The Green Lizard according to locals) is now "Blackbeard's Revenge" and pirates of all ages plunder Nassau Harbour four times a day!

140

On departure day morning, I returned to Potters Cay for one last schedule verification, leaving my luggage at the Colony Club for the Crew to bring later.

Finding no schedule changes, I walked the docks and talked to crews to get ideas for future trips. The *M/V Current Pride* had just docked and I chatted with Captain and part owner Patrick Neilly. Arriving at Potters Cay from Eleuthera's farm country, a dockside produce sale ensued within minutes. Built in St. Augustine in 1980, *Current Pride* is the last wooden mailboat. Closing in on her first half century, she shows no hint of quitting.

Great Harbour Cay:

After collecting the rest of the crew at Stingray Point, a little pub and eatery along the Potters Cay access road, we returned to the docks and loaded aboard *M/V Captain Gurth Dean* around 6:30 pm. We had no problem getting one of the six-person bunk rooms. First in, we selected our bunks and were eventually joined by only one other, a nice young guy who spoke no English but was always smiling. His language was hard to decipher, but sounded a little French. We thought he was probably Haitian as there are many in The Bahamas.

Leaving well past dark, we got a wonderful

141

nighttime view of Nassau Harbour. Early to bed as usual, I slept like a baby, except the 2 am bathroom break was a bit more adventurous than usual. I was up early for the sunrise, but cloud cover disturbed the view. We docked in Bullock's Harbour in Great Harbour Cay about 7 am, having coffee and breakfast after arrival.

A 9 pm departure treated us to a nighttime view of Nassau Harbour.

Crew Perry tries out his bunk!

It was at this dock that I first got the idea to "cruise by mailboat" while watching the *Gurth Dean* unload during a 2012 sailing trip through the area. The event is depicted in the Forward to this book.The *Gurth Dean* trip had long been on my must do list. Not only was Great Harbour Cay mailboat ground zero for me, the Nassau-Sandy Point route was the original route of Ernest Dean Sr's *Captain Dean I,* which started the Dean family mailboat dynasty.

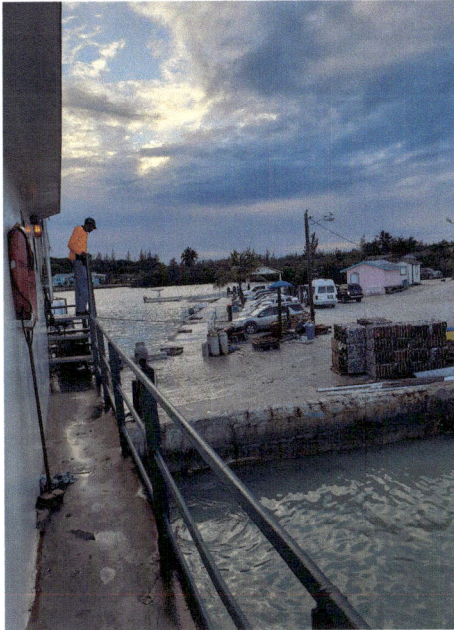

Gurth Dean's Captain Cliff Carroll directs the docking in Bullock's Harbour, Great Harbour Cay.

The night departure was perfect for the Nassau - Great Harbour leg of this trip as its duration almost perfectly coincided with normal sleep time. On mailboats, if Ole Sol doesn't wake you up, mailboat commotion will as most trips are timed for an early morning arrival. Such was the case this trip and we got an early start to our day. We left the boat almost immediately after docking and were off to explore the island on foot. The small town of Bullock's Harbour is on the northwestern part of Great Harbour Cay. We walked the couple of miles length of the island. I looked for the ruins of the "Rat Pack's" beach lodge that is somewhere along the road. I don't know how much time Frank, Peter, Sammy and Dean actually spent here, but they had a place and there are locals hoping that someone will restore it to its former splendor and make it a tourist attraction. It's hard to believe that such a group would pick Great Harbour, about as far from Las Vegas as you can get! We finally landed at the Great Harbour Cay Marina where I had stayed a week on my sloop *Rhombus* both in 2012 and 2018. During my 2012 trip I entered the marina under sail with a busted engine. This trip, I immediately sought out the conveniently located end slip the marina had assigned to my "powerless" boat and relived the terror of the incident. In my nearly forty-year sailing career, the event remains a one of a kind - *knock on wood!*

The Great Harbour Cay Marina is a wonderful sailing stop. (photo by George Kassabgi)

Brown's Garden was a must on my three trips to Bullock's Harbour.

The marina was generous with their WiFi code and my crew stayed for awhile to use it to call home. I hitched a ride back to town. In the Bahamas, all you need to do is put your hand out and if there is room, people will stop. Back in town I went to Brown's Garden for lunch, renewing my acquaintance with Ronnie Brown as I had visited on prior stops. I then toured the R. N. Gomez All Ages School, talked with Principal Father Haynes and visited with students. I was surprised to learn that the school has 160 students aged from three to seventeen and 16 faculty. A few students were Abaco kids who came to Great Harbour for school due to

144

hurricane damage at home. They were easily welcomed into the community.

The older students were on a lunch break and happy to chat.

Later we all reconvened at the mailboat dock and watched the last of the loading. I also chatted with Captain Carroll. From Long Island, he was fairly new on board and had been a captain of boats since about age fifteen. It's a common life routine in the Bahamas, as men who end up operating these boats all seem to start learning their trade at a very young age. Captain Carroll gave me the scoop on the rest of the trip. Sandy Point would be our next stop, bypassing for a time Moore's Island, a remote island located in the bight between Grand Bahama and Great Abaco. I'll probably never get there as chances to go to Moore's Island don't pop up every day!

Sandy Point, Great Abaco Island:

With the change in plans, we would arrive in Sandy Point early the next morning rather than later that evening if we had gone to Moore's Island first. The weather was expected to deteriorate and foul weather was headed our way from the south. Since we were headed north, we hoped that we would beat it. Once in

145

Sandy Point, there would be no more boats in our immediate future as we would be long taxi and airplane rides from home. The sea state was a little bumpy immediately after leaving port but the ride to Sandy Point was better than expected. One member of our Crew did suffer a little until a boat crewman came to the rescue with a magic elixir!

The *Gurth Dean* arrived in Sandy Point just at sunrise and was soon tied up and handling cargo. After saying goodbye to new friends, we left the boat and started walking toward our hotel, Oeisha's Resort. As usually happens in the Bahamas, a kind lady stopped to pick us up and drove us the half mile to the hotel. We were met by Ruth Roberts who showed us to our room. Oeisha's Hotel is a simple and pleasant place and on this visit was populated mostly by young people on a break from volunteering to help repair hurricane damaged homes and businesses.

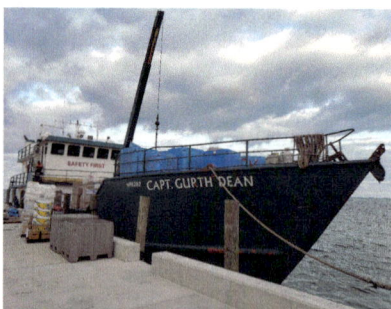

M/V Captain Gurth Dean at the Sandy Point, Abaco Dock during a dawn arrival, as usual!

The change in the mailboat schedule gave us an unexpected full day to explore Sandy Point. Located on the Southwestern corner in a very rural part of Great Abaco Island, Sandy Point is far from the island's tourist centers. It was also the home of Captain Ernest Dean, patriarch of the Dean family and father of the various Dean Shipping Companies operating today. Members of the Dean family still live there and one son occupies the Dean family home. Also still operating is the E & E Grocery Store, the first Dean enterprise founded by Ernest and his wife Eula. Though I had met members of the the Dean family that had migrated to Nassau to run the modern Dean companies, there were Sandy Point Deans I had not met. After checking in at the hotel, I went off to find them. In tiny Sandy Point, members of an iconic family were easy to find. Within a couple of hours, I would meet them all giving me plenty of time to enjoy the rest of the small town. More on my visit with the Sandy Point Deans later.

With a main objective of my visit satisfied, I wandered around town chatting with anybody interested in having a conversation with a stranger from Florida. In The Bahamas that includes about everybody. I also sought out a nice place for dinner and settled on Nancy's Seaside Restaurant, just down the beach from the government pier. Though in between lunch and dinner hours, Nancy's still had some folks to talk to as did the house next door. The location also offered a good vantage point to see the Disney cruise ship *"Fantasy"* docked at Castaway Cay, formerly Gorda Cay before the cruise line took it over to convert to an "island experience" for passengers. Area residents support these arrangements for the jobs they provide, but some lamented the loss of the "best damn fishing island in the area!"

Having had a full day to tour Sandy Point on the day of our arrival, Perry and I moved on to our second

Abaco destination, Little Harbour near Cherokee and across the island on the east coast of Great Abaco. Olga remained in Sandy Point until her departure home by air. With no commercial transportation, Ruth from the hotel offered to drive us the fifty miles or so to Little Harbour. En route we took a quick side tour to Crossing Rocks, just off the highway. In prior days, before automobiles and roads became prevalent in Great Abaco in the 1990s, people traveled from town to town by boat. Great Abaco is a big island and it was a long sail from east to west coasts. Crossing Rocks marked the eastern end of a path that crossed Abaco at its narrowest point. Rather than make the long sail around and passing through the open ocean, people would sail their dinghies to the narrow crossing, hike to the other side of the island, and then often take another boat to one of the communities to the north. Ernest Dean's future wife Eula was from Cherokee just north of Crossing Rocks. He made the trip often.

Bahamian Interlude - The Dean Family of Sandy Point

Mailboats in the Bahamas have been family affairs with several families engaged in the trade for decades, up to and including today. None have been more involved than the Dean family of Sandy Point. Sandy Point lies on the shallow southwestern shore of Great Abaco Island. It is a lightly populated rural area where subsistence farming and fishing have for generations been the main means of support. Born in 1915, Ernest was the oldest of four children of James Alexander and Leah Hunt Dean. Nobody knows for certain when Sandy Point was established, but like other black communities in the Bahamas, establishment may have come shortly after the British Emancipation in 1838. Ernest Dean

148

believed that his great-grandparents were born there, putting the Dean family in Sandy Point near Abaco's modern beginning. Ernest married his wife Eula in 1936 and they would have 12 children of their own. A daughter died as a young child and a son, Gurth was killed in Nassau in the 1990s.

Entrepreneurial from the start, the Deans started a small grocery in a closet in their home. It eventually grew into the E & E Grocery that a second generation of Deans now operates.

Captain Ernest Dean Sr.

Ernest Dean was the patriarch of his generation of the Dean family. Becoming the captain of his dad's fishing boat Champion at age seventeen, he would remain Captain Dean for the next seventy-eight years. In 1949 he constructed the forty-foot, sloop-rigged auxiliary Captain Dean in Sandy Point by hand, without electricity and taking over two years to build.

Initially motivated by the need to obtain regular supplies of milk for his infant children and taking advantage of the recently passed 1948 Mailboat Act, Dean convinced authorities to grant him the mailboat

This lovely Sandy Point beach was once the "shipyard" where the Captain Dean I was built.

contract for service between Sandy Point and Nassau. He eventually added more locations to his route, including Great Harbour Cay in the Berry Islands and Moore's Island, an island to the west of Sandy Point. The Captain Dean I alternated between mailboat and fishing boat for a number of years with Dean's oldest son James serving as captain during the boat's fishing days. Ernest would eventually build six more mailboats named Dean and also acquired several others. When discussing the naming of his boats, Captain Dean wrote in his memoir:

"What I really wanted was something that would put my family name to the front: my name, my father's name for what he taught me, and my sons' name. I finally settled on Captain Dean."

The Dean family is still very much in the mailboat business. Captain Ernst Dean Jr. owns the Dean Shipping Company that operates the M/V Legacy that sails between Nassau and Marsh Harbour on Great Abaco Island and to nearby cays. Dean also operates Champion III in the charter trade between West Palm

Beach and the Florida Keys and throughout the Caribbean. Brothers James and Jonathan operate M/Vs Mia Dean and Gurth Dean respectively. Dean grandchildren are now involved in the family business, extending the Dean legacy another generation.

Captain Ernest Dean Jr. with the author. The MailBoat Gurth Dean operates on Ernest Sr's original mailboat route and sparked my interest in mailboat travel. Shown here with her owner, Captain Jonathan Dean.

Grandson Myron Dean in front of a modern Dean Mailboat "Legacy," aptly named in honor of a great family tradition.

No review of the Dean family and their impact on mailboat history would be complete without a trip to their ancestral home in Sandy Point. Making the short walk into town from the Government Dock, I passed the E & E Grocery. How many passing Floridians would know the store's history? I stopped in the store for a look and immediately found Caroline. She and sister Shirley, both Dean daughters, now operate the store. Shirley was off the island, but Caroline and I had a nice chat. Although Caroline was

Decades past the half century mark, E & E Grocery continues to serve the residents of Sandy Point.

educated off the island from middle school to university in Boston, she happily returned to rural and sleepy Sandy Point to live, remembering her idyllic days as a child. In contrast, her father had been sent to live with a lighthouse keeper as a youth who taught him the 3Rs. Times changed quickly for the Deans. One thing hasn't changed - the Deans' entrepreneurial drive and desire to serve others that led to their remarkable family success.

Dean Shipping Company, Nassau: Right to Left: Myron Dean (Ernest's Grandson), Paulette Fox, Cecily Dean (Ernest's Granddaughter), Kendra Whylly, Salomie Gibson (Ernest's Daughter), Ernelia Dean-Turnquest (Ernest's Granddaughter).

I also talked with Marcus Dean in the family home. He was seven when Ernest Sr. built the Captain Dean I. Marcus had several business careers and operated family boats. He knew St. Augustine, Florida well as several Dean boats were built at the St Augustine

Shipyard and he rode them back to Nassau. Like many in these islands, he went to Nassau to make some money and then returned home. This is a familiar Out-Island story throughout the Bahamas.

Marcus Dean lives in the Dean family home.

By any measure, the Deans have been an extraordinary family and there is a lot of evidence to suggest that their multi-generational success will continue far into the future. Captain Ernest Dean's career spanned over seventy years. He was honored by the Bahamian Government for his service on two occasions, receiving the "Queen's Medal" from the Governor-General of The Bahamas in 1988 and the "British Empire Medal" in 1995. He lived to see his "legacy" intact. He died in 2010 at age 95.

The life and times of Captain Ernest Dean are captured in the memoir "Island Captain," available from White Sound Press.

Little Harbour:

Perry and I arrived at Little Harbour about mid-day and reported to Pete's Pub, focal point of activity in the tiny community. We sought out Amber who would show us the vacation home we had rented. The rental cottage called "The Captain" is located on a ridge with upper and lower porches and panoramic views of the Atlantic Ocean, Little Harbour and the Southern Sea of Abaco just beyond the harbor. After selecting our bedrooms and dumping off our stuff, we walked the beach road to Pete's Pub for an overdue lunch. Too late for a big lunch if I wanted dinner, I opted for cookies and cream pie!

Little Harbour and the Southern Sea of Abaco in the background. I sailed here twice in my trusty sloop Rhombus.

Crew Perry scopes out our gorgeous view and a passing sailboat!

While we were having lunch, an elderly lady, her daughter and grandson approached and asked to share our picnic table. Learning they were from Marsh Harbour, I happened to ask how the "Cottman's Castle" had fared in the storm. Surprised that I knew of it, the conversation led to Cottman himself. Amaryllis Key turned out to be Dr. Robert Stratton's granddaughter. Stratton was the doctor that had recruited Evans Cottman to become the *"Out-Island Doctor,"* whose history is briefly described earlier in this book. His Marsh Harbour home, his "castle," survived!

I enjoyed three idyllic days in Little Harbour. My Crew had departed a day earlier, but I had one last day to work on my notes and savor this special place. With a little time before departure, I hiked to the ocean side visiting the north beach and the ruins of the old lighthouse station. It was established in 1889 at the entrance to Little Harbour Bar. Originally, the lighthouse keeper and his family were the only inhabitants of Little Harbour. Lighthouse families were later joined by the Johnston family. I also got a chance to talk with "Pete," and relived with him his early childhood days as a six-year-old crew on his family's schooner, *Langosta*.

156

On day three, low lying clouds finally cooperated and I got an ocean sunrise from my bedroom porch!

Little Harbour Light Station Ruins

After a delightful last day, I met Marjorie, my pre-arranged ride to the Marsh Harbour Airport and MailBoat III was over. While we covered the dozen miles to the airport, I pondered **"where next?"**

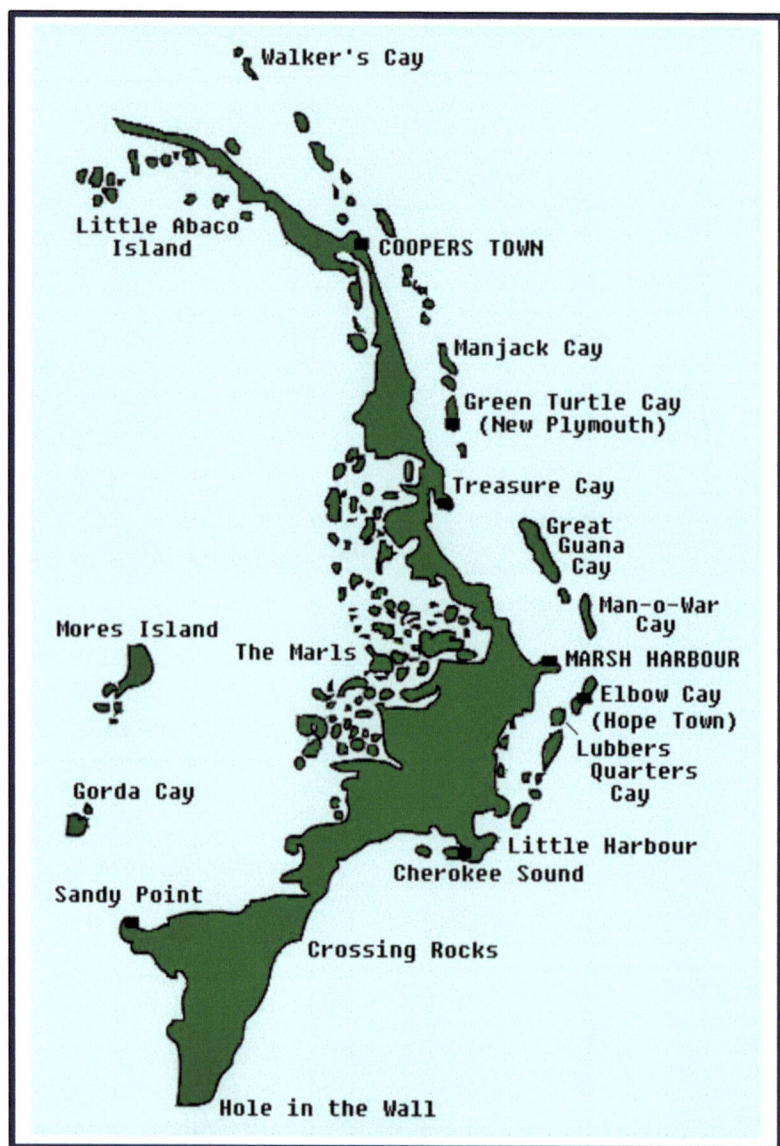

The eastern shore of Great Abaco Island marks the western edge of the Sea of Abaco, a favored cruising area. The smaller cays just to the east form part of the fourth largest barrier reef in the world.

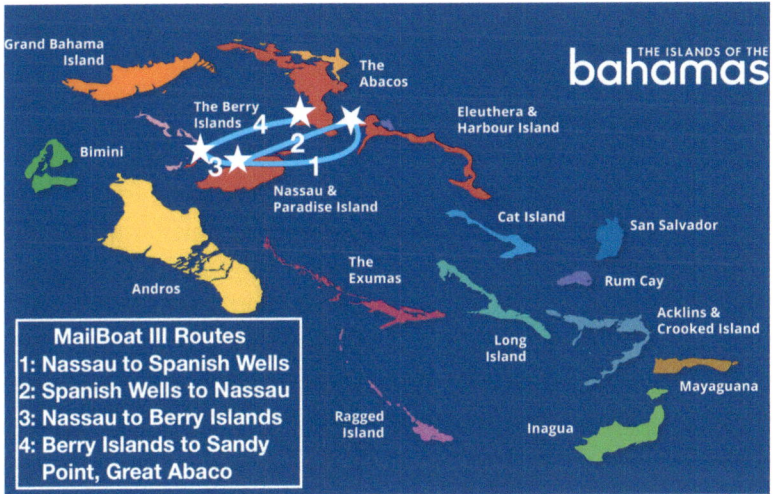

MailBoat III Routes
1: Nassau to Spanish Wells
2: Spanish Wells to Nassau
3: Nassau to Berry Islands
4: Berry Islands to Sandy
   Point, Great Abaco

MailBoat III was unique as it happened just about like our initial plan. Maybe we're getting better at this! We'll see!

Chapter 12: Trips I'd Like to Take

After seven mailboat excursions, seventeen islands and many dozens of Bahamian communities visited, it's time to record what I have learned for others to consider for themselves. Yet there is plenty left to do! The far south, particularly, is in the cross-hairs for future mailboat adventures and somehow popular Cat Island has been missed. The Blue Holes of Andros Island, Delectable Bay on Acklins, Binnacle Hill or Betsy Bay on Mayaguana, the Great Inagua National Parks, and even Cottman's Gun Bluff and the birthplace of mailboats on Crooked Island, all deserve exploration. A second chance at Moore's Island and its small town of Hard Bargain might even pop up. The Bimini Islands deserve a look even though a flight to Nassau and an overnight boat to North Bimini isn't the most efficient way to get to an island forty-three miles from Miami! But, hopefully you are convinced by now that mailboating has never been about travel efficiency! For this author, here are a few future trip possibilities that stand out. Trips for mailboat beginners are covered in the next chapter.

Ragged Island and Exuma Cays: This trip got strong consideration for MailBoat III and is first on my personal list for the long trip to the far south. Located about 180 miles from Nassau and 60 miles from Cuba, this route is currently serviced by *M/V Captain "C,"* and has a different routine than most mailboat operations. Rather than unloading cargo and loading new cargo at each stop, on this route cargo is staged only for off-load in the Exuma Cays en route to Ragged Island. The boat picks up Nassau bound cargo on the return trip. The boat remains overnight at an Exuma Cay in both directions and at Ragged Island, giving travelers time to explore their surroundings at three locations in one trip.

But, this trip is a serious mailboat commitment; three plus days and three nights on board, and won't be recommended for mailboat rookies until I do it myself!

Current Pride and Northern Eleuthera: This trip is for the love of the history, as Current Pride has been in the trade for over forty years and is the last wooden mailboat. She travels to the farm country I have been to before, stopping at three locations including Current Island. It's a daytime trip until stopping in her North Eleuthera home in the tiny town of The Bluff for a few days before returning to Nassau. Varying stays in the area are possible with earlier returns by mailboats serving nearby Spanish Wells, short land and water taxi rides away. It was never on my list until I visited the boat, chatted with its owner/captain, and observed the large number of "farmer passengers" with their produce cargo to sell. A chatty crowd, they seemed to be having so much fun and the trip promises to be a great afternoon of conversation!

Cat Island: Cat Island, after serving a stint as San Salvador, was named after the pirate Arthur Catt, and has been influential in Bahamian culture. The first European settlers on Cat Island were Loyalists fleeing the American Revolution in 1783 with their slaves. Sir Sidney Poitier grew up amongst the island's rolling hills and pink sand beaches. No one, especially of my vintage, will forget *Guess Who's Coming to Dinner; To Sir, with Love and In the Heat of the Night.* The Sidney Poitier Bridge connects Nassau and Paradise Island and towers over Potters Cay in the process. Another contribution to world culture has its roots on Cat Island. *"Rake 'N' Scrape"* music took form on the island with instruments made from everyday objects like raking handsaws are added to traditional instruments of banjo,

161

drums and guitar, and dates back to the culture of enslaved ancestors. Cat Island entertainer Tony Mackay, also called Exuma and the "Obeah Man," exported his homegrown music around the world. Almost unclassifiable, the music is a strong mixture of carnival, Junkanoo, calypso, reggae, African and folk. Although quite rural with a population of under two thousand, the fifty-mile-long island is a popular cruising destination and will have its share of boaters and tourist activities. Included is an annual "Rake 'N' Scrape" Festival in June of each year. Served by mailboats to the island's northern and southern tips, an island-long tour seems a likely plan.

Andros Island: Having failed in three attempts to visit Andros, twice by sail and once by mailboat, the island is high on my personal list. Andros is the largest island in the Bahama Archipelago and the fifth-largest in the Caribbean. With a population density of three residents per square mile, Andros is almost uninhabited and the true outback of the Bahamas. The island is sliced up by a network of creeks, wetlands and shallow flats. The West Side National Park overflows with bonefish and creates shelter for a thriving pink flamingo population. Pine forests in central Andros shelter migratory birds, along with hundreds of inland blue holes. South and North Andros are served by multiple mailboats and, with trip durations of five to seven hours, Andros is one of the mailboat destinations closest to Nassau. Andros is a large island, and unlike most Bahama Islands, has lots of fresh water; bring mosquito repellant.

Chapter 13: MailBoating in Practice
Trips and Tips for MailBoat Rookies

There are some advantages in getting old! Not many, but some. One of the advantages is not being too influenced by time and a definite schedule. Admittedly, time flexibility is a nice thing when it comes to mailboat travel. But, for the adventurous at heart regardless of age or career situation, there may be a mailboat trip for you.

Who Should go "MailBoating?"

Although I am a true MailBoat "evangelist," who among <u>you</u> stands the best chance of looking back on a trip with fond memories? My wife is an experienced world traveler, but I wouldn't dream of asking her to come along. So then, who should go and what travel understanding should they take with them? Here are a few categories of folks who stand a good chance of enjoying the experience:

* Campers, boaters and backpackers
* Hikers and walkers
* Travelers with a clear understanding that:
    - as an adventure, everything may not be perfect
    - it will not be enormously expensive, but not cheap either
    - form travel groups who know each other well
    - have an escape plan for crew members that have had enough fun
    - consider the possibility of motion sickness

* Young and old, male or female. Anyone who fits into some of the above categories should do well.

Mailboat travel is certainly not for everyone, but if you can tolerate some travel uncertainty, it can lead to memorable experiences. It certainly has for me and my fellow travelers. You will visit some really nice places well off the beaten path. You generally won't encounter too many mega-resorts while traveling among the mostly rural Out-Islands. However, on one trip we did end up at a Club Med, rare indeed with mailboat travel! Some places have one or two hundred residents, a small town with a grocery and a hardware store that may also serve breakfast, maybe a shop that caters to the few tourists, and always a bar and restaurant. But, there is always a great beach on one side of the island and scenic rocky cliffs on the other. You'll also find a small hotel or at least someone who will rent rooms and possibly even an "in-shore blue hole," where diving records can be set. Wherever, you will certainly find delightful Bahamians with which to swap stories and they'll swap, just give them a hint that you are interested. Bahamians seem shy, but they are very open people if you give them an entree. So, if you are a traveler who can find fun anywhere and appreciate the little places, then there are many choices. There is an allure in traveling to destinations on absolutely nobody's bucket list. If you are just a tad more discriminating, there are still a lot of choices that provide the true flavor of the Out-Islands, yet have a little more in-town life.

Mailboat Travel Strategy

From experience, a few MailBoat travel strategies emerge for various traveler categories in terms of time constraints and location preferences.

Traveler characteristics determine a planning direction. A few recommendations are thrown in.

Caribbean Equivalent of European Backpackers: For Mailboaters with oodles of time, enough money and a desire to see what they can see, no strategy is required. Just go!!

Flexible Schedule Travelers with Some Constraints: Most of us land here. Though all but one of my fellow travelers were retired with generally very flexible schedules, we all had constraints. The most operative constraint is the airline reservation. Except for one instance (mailboat travel to Freeport and ferry to Florida), mailboat trips begin and end in Nassau. Even if you end up flying home from an island, virtually all flights from the Out-Islands travel through Nassau regardless of the final destination. It's always possible to fly to Nassau from any Bahama Island. So, coming from the United States, a mailboat excursion is the most cost-effective with a round-trip airplane ticket to Nassau. The in-between period of whatever length is available for mailboats and will be left to experience, but the start and stop dates are known.

Multi-Island Travelers: Mailboat travelers who want to visit several islands, spend at least a few days to explore each, and still keep some semblance of a schedule will usually incorporate some air transportation into their plans. Mailboats usually arrive at an island early in the morning and ordinarily depart by evening for another island or a return to Nassau. Regardless, the next mailboat is a week away, leaving the traveler with two choices for mailboat only travel: spend little time exploring your destination or spend a week doing it. The alternate is to spend three or four days at a location, usually plenty of time, and fly to a nearby island for a few days before returning to Nassau, by mailboat if possible. Our first trip was to Long Island and after a few great days, we took "Freddy Air" to nearby San Salvador for another great stay. None of it was planned!

Single Island Traveler: Plan on a week at every island. Most islands have weekly, round-trip Nassau-island-Nassau mailboat schedules. This is the simplest approach, although it may restrict possible destinations to those that offer a week's worth of exploring. I'm one who loves seeing different places and am always glad for the experience. However, many people would prefer more to do to fill a week than some locations offer. This is a great choice for those mailboaters who want to fly to Nassau, board a mailboat, enjoy an out-island week, return on a mailboat and fly home from Nassau or repeat the routine for a second destination.

Travelers to Eleuthera: Eleuthera travelers can be from any of the above categories. The Fast Ferry mailboats travel almost daily to Eleuthera, most often to the northern end which includes not only mainland Eleuthera, but also nearby islands of Spanish Wells and Harbour Island. Their schedules are set and not subject to the variability of the smaller mailboats. Smaller, traditional mailboats also service both of the two northern islands and other parts of mainland Eleuthera. For a time-limited trip, or even an open-ended one, Eleuthera is a great choice. It is the best-served island by boats of all descriptions with frequent, daily, water-taxi transportation between the mainland, Harbour Island and Spanish Wells. All three are terrific places to visit and are very different from each other. With one cab and a couple of water-taxi rides, you can visit all three, although readily available rental cars are required to explore the mainland. A little of everything for "islanders" of all persuasions, the area is hard to beat. On one MailBoat trip, we took a ferry to mainland Eleuthera, spent the night, then took a cab to the water-taxi dock en route to Harbour Island the next day. After a few days there, we took the MailBoat to Spanish Wells, stayed a few days, then took the MailBoat back to Nassau. Some variation of this trip is available almost every day.

Other Well-Connected Islands: Just a little pre-trip research will identify other well-connected island locations. These locations are often served by more frequent departures and offer trip scheduling options not available in smaller and more rural islands and cays. They will most often also be the more developed of the Out-Islands. Besides Eleuthera, this is a short list of MailBoat destinations that provide transportation advantages and a little about them. I am certain that this is an incomplete list, but only trips I have made personally are considered here:

Marsh Harbour and the Abaco Islands: This is a personal favorite and well worth a lengthy visit. Marsh Harbour is the main town and commercial hub of the Abaco Islands Region and is regularly served by both traditional and Fast Ferry MailBoats. It is a delightful place and is close to smaller cays that line the barrier reef to the east and across the Sea of Abaco from Marsh Harbour. Since you've read this book, you already know their names: Hope Town on Elbow Cay, Great Guana Cay, Man-O-War Cay, and Little Harbour, just down the Island. The outer cays are reachable by people-shuttles that operate throughout the day. From one base, you can see them all. Green Turtle Cay is a little more distant, but reachable with a cab ride and another people ferry. Treasure Cay is reachable by taxi from Marsh Harbour. Both destinations are well worth the effort.

Georgetown and Great Exuma Island: Great Exuma Island and its main center of Georgetown are also served by multiple mailboat lines. A yachting favorite, there is plenty to do in town and while exploring Great and Little Exuma Islands and near-by Stocking Island. The area is well worth a week's stay.

Long Island: Like the above two destinations, Long Island is also served by both traditional and Fast Ferry MailBoats. Long Island is a long way from Nassau, and the small traditional mailboats may well go elsewhere on the scheduled day if a good cargo load to another island happens their way. Long Island is a *long island*. It is mostly rural and the small towns are really small. Beach combing is the best and there's the Blue Hole and enough party spots to keep the evenings occupied. However, after four or five days you may wish to move on to a nearby island. For us, San Salvador was the answer, and "Freddy Air" was the way!

San Salvador: Site of the initial landing of the first Bahamas cruiser, San Salvador has much more to offer for a week's stay than a hike to the Columbus Monument. Once named Watlings Island after another area pirate, San Salvador is half the size and has a third of the population of Long Island. It has the usual beautiful beaches, considerable island activity, and offers plenty of diversions to consume a week's stay. There is also a Club Med if you can figure out a way to visit! Check out one of the several charming mom and pop hotels that dot the island.

Travel Planning

Ok, you're convinced - a MailBoat trip is for you! What next? You already know a lot, but some research of the latest information and some final cautions are in order before selecting a departure:

Information Gathering:

MailBoat travel is an imperfect science, which is part of its charm. There is a lot of information on-line and it is getting to be more reliable, at least for the most traveled destinations. While I hesitate to provide actual URLs as they change, there are searches that will bring up a wide range of the latest information available. Some searches you might try:

* Official Travel Site of The Bahamas
* Bahamas Guru
* Bahamas Travel Mailboat Schedule
* Bahamas Ferries Schedule
* The MailBoat Company
* Dean Shipping Company
* Marine Historian Eric Wiberg

Search these sites and with a few clicks you'll get enough information to fill in the blanks in a plan, remembering that in mailboat travel a plan is just a starting point! The MailBoat III Plan is in the appendix as an example.

Note: Hurricanes are a reality in The Bahamas. Although islands always work hard to recover their place as prime tourist destinations after any storm, any trip plan must consider the effects of recent storm damage. Pre-trip planning can reveal the current status of any area.

Additionally, The Bahamas covers a large area of ocean. Storms never hit all of the country and there are always multiple available destinations.

Suggested Trip Itinerary

Nassau: MailBoat trips start and end in Nassau. Our mailboat crews have come from various parts of the country, all arriving on a Saturday, planning to stay a few nights before the first MailBoat trip. Nassau can be fun and some of our great adventures occurred while traveling around New Providence Island, on which Nassau sits. So, go to Nassau at least a day or two before your planned initial mailboat departure, allowing plenty of time to acclimate to the surroundings and check out what's ahead.

Potters Cay: First up after collecting the crew in Nassau is checking out MailBoat Heaven, Potters Cay. It's worth the trip in itself! Buy a six-pack, find a bench, and watch the choreographed commotion for a while. Then wander the docks, see where the boats are berthed, find the various mailboat ticket offices, and talk to any mailboat crews that you may encounter for scheduling intelligence that they may offer. You might even be invited aboard for a quick look. For certain, stop by the Potters Cay Dockmaster's office to get the latest mailboat schedule. In spite of your on-line work, there will be some surprises and maybe a change of plans. It was there that we learned that the *Captain Moxey* wasn't leaving on the day scheduled and the *Cape Mail* to Cat Island didn't take passengers. We ended up on different islands both times. *Ahh, mailboat travel!*

Early Week Departures: Monday through Wednesday are the best days for planned departures. Almost all of the traditional mailboat designated vessels depart then and return late in the week or on weekends. The Fast Ferries operate on most days throughout the week, including weekends. Our favorite departure day is Tuesday, allowing time on Monday to check with the Dockmaster to get the latest schedule, chat with crews while they get the boats ready, and make a new plan if necessary.

General Trip Information

Accommodations: When you are not positive exactly where you are going, where to stay upon arrival is always an issue. On most of our trips we made late on-line reservations at small hotels when we were fairly certain that we knew where we'd end up. The Bahamas Tourist Bureaus were terrific at finding us a place when we arrived "homeless." We can't say enough about the service received at every office we've encountered. Several times we arrived with no idea of where we would spend the night. Once we ended up in a fellow traveler's living room. We also slept on a bus in the owner's driveway when he couldn't find room for us anywhere else. Through it all, we never slept on a beach, though we were prepared to do so.

Experience indicates that you can always find a place to stay in The Bahamas, especially in the Out-Islands. But, you may need to ask. We once arrived at a tiny little town at 8 pm on a Sunday night, thinking that this might be "the beach night." The cab driver who met the mailboat took us to a friend's house and we had a great dinner, comfortable night, and a big family breakfast before departure in the morning. *The experience was the true essence of mailboat travel.* The moral of the story: the Out-Island Bahamians are most accommodating and can always use an unexpected customer. If you need something? Ask! Don't be afraid to approach strangers.

Finances: The cost of a mailboat excursion is a difficult question, but one that is always asked. The short answer is, if you are doing this to save a lot of money, you might reconsider. The mailboats themselves are inexpensive. However, there is no package travel discount here. The small hotels you encounter are not "big US city prices," but not cheap either. There will be lots of transportation costs: car and golf cart rentals, taxis, and an occasional unplanned airplane ride. We are always very generous with the Bahamians who serve and help us. Dollar for dollar, you could easily take a Bahamas cruise for what you'll spend mailboating. The experience, however, will be much different. As an added note, the Bahamian dollar is on a par with the US dollar and are used interchangeably. Credit cards can be used for many hotels, car rentals, airline tickets, the Fast Ferries and some mailboats. ATM machines are available at most banks, but it's best to try out your debit card early after arrival and before you need it. Always notify your provider beforehand. If forced to put a number on a trip, maybe $1,200 per person per week would be in the ballpark depending on how closely your spending habits mirror ours. We didn't cut corners and drank a lot of beer!

What to Take: Travel light! Rather than using large backpacks, most mailboat travelers used an airplane carry-on sized roller bag with two wheels. We do a lot of walking. Find an old one with good wheels as it will be much older when you return. The four wheeled models don't work as well. Some travelers also took a small backpack to use around town and for essentials when bags are palletized as cargo while on the boats. In addition to the usual personal items, here are a few things to consider:

   * Motion sickness medication - mailboats are not small craft, but they aren't cruise ships either. They are also necessarily shallow-draft vessels and feel the sea state. A few of the collective "crew" felt some unease on occasion. Know your tendencies and prepare ahead of time.
   * Layered clothing - only the most casual clothes needed. Laundry service is easy to find, even if it's from a willing neighbor.

   * Biker's style sleeping bag that rolls up into a small ball. Mailboats usually provide sheets and pillows with cases, but rarely blankets and often only a bottom sheet. My bag unzipped to form a light blanket, or I could crawl into it on those cool evenings at sea. I was often glad I had it.

Going and Have Questions? Like all the people mentioned who have helped me, I'm happy to help you. If you think you would like to make a trip, send me a note: *fredbraman@hotmail.com*. I'll get back to you.

Appendix A
Mailboat Trip Planning

Note: Our MailBoat I plan was simple. Let's go! We did check on-line mailboat schedules and had only a general idea of what we wanted to do, none of which worked as planned. By the time MailBoat III came around a couple of years later, the plan got more detailed. Below is the plan for MB III as a sample for trip organizers. It didn't all work, but most of it did. This plan was written for a new MailBoat Crew, and was designed to educate as well as provide trip details.

MailBoat III Plan

It's time to go mailboating!!! After some research, here's a plan. Departure is on February 15, 2020. Exact return date TBA, but I anticipate about 7-20 days depending on the departure return option selected.

General Plan: Two trips are planned. To provide maximum scheduling flexibility for an early return if desired, Eleuthera is the first destination. Crew can return home after Trip I if they wish. Eleuthera is easiest for individual crew to have their own return date. It is close to Nassau (2-5 hour day trips depending on the boat) and is served by boat daily on the return and every day except Tuesday on the way over from Nassau. There is also daily air. Sandy Point is less written about in the travel literature. I'm not certain what we will find in Sandy Point and whether it will be enough for everyone or can it accommodate a large group. South Abaco doesn't present the scheduling flexibility regarding the return as does Eleuthera and is best selected as a second destination for those with flexible schedules. Trip details follow.

Trip I: Northern Eleuthera

At its very north end, Eleuthera includes two islands: Spanish Wells (NW corner of the mainland) and Harbour Island (NE corner). The mainland itself is connected to the two islands by water taxi. For decades Spanish Wells did not bother with tourists, but now has some tourist facilities.

A Spanish Wells - Mainland Eleuthera split, and maybe a day in Harbour Island looks like a good plan. The mainland has a lot; many neat little towns plus the Island School and Eleuthera Institute. The institute studies sustainable living and the school teaches it to high school kids from around the world.

Trip II: Berry Islands, Sandy Point and South Abaco

The *M/V Captain Gurth Dean* is the target boat. I watched her unload in Great Harbour Cay during my 2012 sailing cruise through the islands. I saw her again six years later in the same spot.

This trip will be full circle for me. This is the original Ernest Dean Senior route. As always, we start in Nassau at Potters Cay. The boat leaves on Tuesday evenings at 6 PM. She always goes to Great Harbour first and stays there most of the day Wednesday, giving us some time to see the island. The next stop depends on the tides. *Gurth Dean* requires more water than Sandy Point offers at low tide or close to it. So, depending on the tides, the boat may go to Moore's Island first. Either way, we will get to Sandy Point Thursday. Moore's is a little island. I suspect we'll have a little time to walk around it a bit and "possibly" grab a beer or two!

Sandy Point and Beyond: Sandy Point is a small town. It is the ancestral home of the Dean Family. Ernest Sr believed that his great grandparents lived there putting the family among the earliest of the modern Bahamas settlers. The little grocery store he and his wife started before he went mailboating is still operating. A couple of his daughters operate it now. Plan to stay 2-3 days. I'm researching places now. This is a fishing center for anyone who'd like to try it.

Sometime while we are there, we need to figure out how to get a car so we can easily tour the southern part of Great Abaco. This will be new territory for me. The shallow waters in the little bays on both sides of the island always kept me away while traveling by sailboat. I haven't been south of Little Harbour (Pete's Pub). I'm researching places to hang a few days while we explore. Two possibilities are the little cottages that Pete rents in Little Harbour and a small lodge called Sandpiper, located near Crossing Rocks. They will pick us up in Sandy Point and will find us a rental car. I'm sure there are others. (A nearby neem farm rents cottages!) There is no car rental in Sandy Point. It's a 50-minute cab ride to the airport at Marsh Harbour and a couple of car rental places are there. We may be able to rent a car from a private owner in Sandy Point. In the Bahamas, there is always a way. If we do go to the airport to get a car, that opens up options for our return. The area in South Abaco was not damaged by the hurricane. I think there will be some great exploring well away from the tourist areas. There is some history to explore and I want to see the lighthouse.

Travel Options: Mailboat history indicates that it is best to arrive in Nassau by Sunday. With mailboat travel, the "schedule" is a bit approximate! Monday is a good day to prowl the docks and talk to crews. Tuesday is the biggest MB departure day and if travel modifications are necessary, it's best to find out on Monday. On our first three MB attempts, we ended up going somewhere different than planned twice. Monday on the docks is a fun day anyway. Arrival on Saturday gives us a little time to enjoy Nassau. But either weekend day will do. The first one in gets the rental car and collects the others upon arrival. It's the return that presents some options:

Travel Summary:

Trip I: Northern Eleuthera

Arrive Nassau Saturday 2/15.
Enjoy the ambiance of Potters Cay 2/16
Depart for Spanish Wells Eleuthera 2/17 on *Bo Hengy* (arrive about noon)
Explore Eleuthera from arrival until selected departure date, probably 2/23 for most. Can split the time between SW and HI or one of the smaller rural towns on the mainland. From sailing through there most recently in 2018, I have some favorite spots!

Those wishing to return home after Eleuthera can easily do so. Also possible to return from Eleuthera by air directly.

Trip II: Berry Islands, Sandy Point and South Abaco

Gurth Dean leaves on a Tuesday and returns on a Friday. Arrival on Thursday gives us up to a week and a day to explore, depending on choices made.

Option 1 All MailBoat: Stay on board *Gurth Dean* for a mailboat round trip. That's five days on a mailboat with stops!!!

2/23 Saturday/Sunday arrival in Nassau from Eleuthera
2/25 Tuesday sail on *Gurth Dean*: Wednesday arrival in Great Harbour Cay in the Berry Islands. Boat stays all day and departs in the evening. Should have time to explore a bit, lunch and grab a cold one. Thursday arrival Sandy Point and Friday night departure from Sandy Point. Will visit Moore's Island if we didn't go there on the way to SP.
Saturday morning arrival in Nassau
3/1 or 3/2 fly home

Option 2 MailBoat - Abaco Stopover - MailBoat

2/23 Saturday/Sunday arrival in Nassau from Eleuthera
2/25 Tuesday sail on *Gurth Dean*
Wednesday arrival in Great Harbour Cay in the Berry Islands
Thursday arrival Sandy Point
2/27-29 Sandy Point
Saturday thru Friday tour South Abaco
3/6 Friday night departure from Sandy Point
Saturday morning arrival in Nassau
3/8 or 3/9 fly home

Option 3: Mailboat - Abaco Stopover - Flight:

2/23 Saturday/Sunday arrival in Nassau from Eleuthera
2/25 Tuesday sail on *Gurth Dean*
Wednesday arrival in Great Harbour Cay in the Berry Islands.
Thursday arrival Sandy Point
2/27-29 Sandy Point
3/1-5 Spend a few days exploring South Abaco and fly home from Marsh Harbour whenever we want.

Note: In South Abaco, the distances are short, and we'll not be more than an hour's taxi ride from MH airport. We should have a rental car and can deliver anyone to the airport about any time. The air travel costs are about the same any way we do it. If we decide on which return to take soon after arrival, I'm sure we can find a way home while retaining lots of flexibility, always a good thing in mailboat travel. We can always get to Nassau and home from there. For those with no schedule requirements, the *M/V Fiesta Mail* can be taken to Freeport and the ferry to Ft. Lauderdale from there. That would add 2-3 days. I don't have a hard date for return. For those of us in east Florida, my take is to buy a one-way ticket to Nassau and let the rest take care of itself. For return, I'm leaning toward a flight home to JAX from Marsh Harbour, but may opt for a MB return to Nassau. West Florida folks might look at Silver Airlines with two one-way trips instead of a round trip.

Early Returners: Crew needing a little shorter trip can arrive on Sunday, stay as long as you want and fly home.

Late Returners: Crew with no time restrictions can take the MailBoat *Fiesta Mail* to Freeport and the ferry to Ft. Lauderdale and fly or catch Amtrak home.

MB III Research

Note: Though reservations are risky to make, the plan included an effort to research as many potential places to stay as we could find for each location that we might visit. The little mom-and-pops are frequently not on-line, but the local Tourist Bureaus know about them. Most of our stays have been discovered as we went. Ideally, we'll want a reserved place for our first stop upon landing: Nassau, Spanish Wells and Sandy Point. For the rest, we can wing it! Having it all wired is not only impossible but will miss some of the fun. If history is a teacher, it probably won't work out like the above, but we'll go somewhere and we'll sleep someplace! Research also included potential return home-by-air possibilities from the most likely locations for use later.

Notes for MailBoat Newbies:

1. Cash. For the big things like airlines and most hotels, credit cards work. We will also encounter ATMs. However, most other things require cash. I took $2000 last trip and brought most of it home with me. We tip generously, so lots of small bills are good. US and Bahamian dollars are spent interchangeably.

2. Group expenses. Invariably, each of us will spend money for the group. Airline and hotel reservations made on the fly with credit cards are most easily paid for by one of us and we try to divide up the payment opportunities. So, we keep track and after the trip we do a big accounting, find an average, and determine who sends money to who. Mailboaters leaving early will not be billed for your post-departure fun!

3. Remember flexibility! To date, MailBoat travel has about a 50 percent success rate of getting to the planned island and on the planned boat, part of its charm. Our very first trip was to nearby Andros Island and we ended up in Long Island hundreds of miles south. Later, headed to Cat Island, we went to Great Exuma instead. Schedule changes happen. This is certain: we'll get somewhere, we'll sleep someplace and it'll be a hoot!

Appendix B
Notes About Mailboat Schedules

As we have learned, mailboat trip scheduling is an imprecise art form. Schedules are available online for the traditional mailboats. They will give you an idea of what goes where, but only as a planning starting point. For example, the official Bahamas site still shows the Eleuthera Express, which was made into a pirate ship venue some time ago. Boat names serving a particular area often change. Boats are occasionally out-of-service for maintenance and overhaul periods and will be replaced on their route by a substitute boat. Although the boat names frequently change, the routes rarely do. Boats often leave a day late, but rarely early. Regardless of frequent changes, the schedules are still helpful for pre-planning. You can call the Dockmaster's Office, but you will only learn about the current week's schedule. An idea of the possibilities plus a willingness to change plans are still keys to happy mailboating.

Schedules for the fast ferries are also on line (probably more accurate), but the method of presentation is different in that you select a departure point and a destination and get sailing times for that pair. There is no "schedule menu" that you can peruse for all sailings at one time. They do have a "route map" to start from while doing preliminary research on line. Full, written schedules are available at the ferry ticket office on Potters Cay. Remember, getting to Nassau a couple of days before the first mailboat departure is key to finalizing a plan. Helpful search suggestions are in Chapter 13.

Bibliography

Eric Wiberg and Steve Dodge, through discussions, talks and written works provided much of the historical information and mailboat details contained in this book. Many others made substantial contributions.

Book references and suggested reading:

1. Dodge, Steve *Abaco, A History of an Out Island and its Cays,* White Sound Press, 2005.
2. Wiberg, Eric, *Mailboats of the Bahamas (scheduled for Sumer 2021 release. Preliminary draft provided by the author).*
3. Dean, Ernest Alexander, *Island Captain,* White Sound Press, 1997.
4. Cottman, Evans W. *Out-Island Doctor,* Media Publishing,1998.
5. Johnston, Randolph W. *Artist on His Island,* Little Harbour Press, 1975.
6. Riley, Sandra, *Homeward Bound,* Parrot House, 2015.
7. Gale, Dave, *Below Another Sky,* Carib Communications, 2011.
8. Gale, Dave, *Ready About,* Carib Communications, 2002.
9. Diedrick, Amanda, *Those Who Stayed,* Little House by the Ferry, 2016.
10. Craton, Michael and Saunders, Gail, *Islanders in the Stream,* Volume 2, University of Georgia Press, 1998.
11. Moran, Joseph M. *Ocean Studies: Introduction to Oceanography,* American Meteorological Society, 2008.

12. Parlett, Lynn, *Doctor Seabreeze's Eleuthera,* Dats The Truth, LLC, 2014
13. Albury, Haziel L. *Man-O-War, My Island Home,* Holly Press, 1977.
14. Barrett, Peter, *Bahama Saga,* 1st Books, 2011. (Kindle Edition)
15. Stark, John H. *Stark's History and Guide to the Bahama Islands,* (Kindle Edition)
16. Higman, B.W. *A Concrete History of the Caribbean,* Cambridge Concise Histories, 2010. (Kindle Edition)
17. Johnson, W.R. *Bahamian Sailing Craft,* White Sound Press, 2000
18. Woodard, Colin, *The Republic of Pirates,* Colin Woodard Harcourt, Inc, 2007
19. Powles, Louis Diston, *Land of the Pink Pearl,* St. Dustin's House, London, 1888

Articles and Research Papers:

1. *Live Science Planet Earth,* World's Deepest Blue Hole Is in South China Sea, Stephanie Pappas, Live Science Contributor | July 27, 2016.
2. *Geology of the Bahamas Final Paper,* by Marion Lytle, Miami University, June 6, 2006.
3. *Published Writings,* by Eric Wiberg, Island Books, 2017.
4. *Geotectonic Evolution and Subsidence of Bahama Platform,* by Dietz, Holden and Sproll, Geo Science World, July 1970.
5. *Saharan Dust,* Science News, July 24, 2014.
6. *Historical Origins of Food Preservation,* by Brian A. Nummer, Ph.D. National Center for Home Food Preservation, May 2002.
7. *Little Harbour is a world away,* Hamilton Spectator, May 09, 2008.

8. *Little Harbour Lighthouse/Rolling Harbour Abaco*: https://rollingharbour.com/lighthouses/little-harbour-lighthouse/
9. *Tony Mackay bio:* http://www.bahamasentertainers.com/Artist/Exuma/exuma_bio.html
10. *Abaco Life*, www.abacolife.com. Volumes 2017-2019.
11. *Journal of the Bahamas Historical Society*, November 2018.
12. *AD 1493: The Pope asserts rights to colonize, convert, and enslave,* National Institutes of Health, Health & Human Services paper, 2015.
13. *SS Laura (1885),* Creative Commons-Wikipedia, November 2019.
14. *Abaco Dinghies*, Randall Peffer, Small Boats Magazine, April 2016.
15. *Johnston's Little Harbour: Artist on His Island,* Andy Schell, All at Sea Magazine, May 19, 2014.
16. *A Genetic History of the Pre-Contact Caribbean*, Daniel Fernandes, Kendra Sirak and David Reich, Nature, 2020.

Interviews, Meetings and Discussions:

1. Talk by Maritime Historian Eric Wiberg, Bahamas Historical Society, Nassau, August 1, 2019.
2. Interview with Steve Dodge, author and historian, New Smyrna Beach, Fl, September 14, 2018.
3. Interview with Andre Sands, lobster fisherman, Spanish Wells, February 24, 2020.
4. Interview with Billy Pinder, 1st owner and captain of the *Eleuthera Express*, now a Pirate Ship attraction in Nassau, Spanish Wells, February 24, 2020.
5. Interview with Captain and owner Patrick Neilly, aboard his MailBoat *Current Pride*, Nassau, February 26, 2020.

6. Interview with Amaryllis Key - Granddaughter of "Dr" Robert Stratton, Little Harbour, February 29, 2020.
7. Interview with Pete Johnston, son of Randolph Johnston, Little Harbour, March 2, 2020.

About the Author

Captain Frederick Braman, USN (ret), lives in Fleming Island, Florida with his wife Louise of over fifty years. High school sweethearts, both are originally from Bay City, Michigan.

Having lived on three continents, the Bramans have traveled the world, much of it during a quarter century long Navy career. They have called several places in Michigan, Tennessee, California, Virginia, Japan and Italy home, before landing in Florida. Following his Navy retirement in 1994, Fred taught high school math for fifteen years in the USA and in Italy. Fred is a graduate of General Motors Institute (now Kettering University) with a B.S. degree in engineering and from the US Naval Post-Graduate School with a M.S. degree in management. Fred and Louise have a daughter Monica Kruse, Son-in-Law Matt, Grandson Grant and Granddaughter Madchen, who fortunately live nearby.

A lifelong sailor, sailing adventures led to Fred's writing as he described his cruises along the US East Coast, Cuba, the Caribbean and throughout the Bahamas over several decades. He has published over fifty magazine articles and his first book, *"Too Old Not to Go,"* chronicled his 2012, two thousand mile, single-handed voyage throughout the main island groups of the Bahamas in his trusty Catalina 30 sloop *Rhombus.* It was on this trip that he first noticed MailBoats.

Fred loves The Bahamas and, in the midst of a wonderful retirement, more adventures are hoped for, both by sail and by MailBoat.